THE WELL-TEMPERED ACCOMPANIST

Coenraad V. Bos

The
WELL-TEMPERED
ACCOMPANIST

by
COENRAAD V. BOS
as told to
Ashley Pettis

THEODORE PRESSER CO.
Bryn Mawr, Pennsylvania

COPYRIGHT 1949
THEODORE PRESSER CO.
British Copyright Secured

To my esteemed friend
Mrs. Melbert B. Cary, Jr., with admiration
for her great knowledge of the fine art of
music.

                    COENRAAD V. BOS

TABLE OF CONTENTS

	PAGE
Foreword	ix

CHAPTER		PAGE
I:	The Accompanist's Background and Equipment	11
II:	The School of Experience	22
III:	Suiting the Action to the Word	37
IV:	Traditions in the Making	48
V:	Beginnings, Endings, and Various Ad Interim Problems	63
VI:	The Well-Tempered Accompanist	78
VII:	The Accompanist as Coach	98
VIII:	Problems of Style	109
IX:	The Human Angle	128
X:	Considering the Public	148

ILLUSTRATIONS

	PAGE
COENRAAD V. BOS	*Frontispiece*
RAIMUND VON ZUR-MÜHLEN	25
MARCELLA SEMBRICH	27
DR. LUDWIG WÜLLNER AND COENRAAD V. BOS	53
HELEN TRAUBEL AND COENRAAD V. BOS	56
POSTCARD FROM RICHARD STRAUSS	56
JULIA CULP	61
ELENA GERHARDT	80
MACK HARRELL AND COENRAAD V. BOS	104
FRIEDA HEMPEL	106
MASTER CLASS BY COENRAAD V. BOS	108
PROGRAM OF RECITAL BY KLARA ERLER	135
POSTCARD FROM JOSEPH JOACHIM	136
PROGRAM OF CONCERT HONORING 60TH BIRTHDAY OF MAX BRUCH	138
PROGRAM OF "DAS HOLLÄNDISCHE TRIO," WITH JOSEPH JOACHIM AND EMANUEL WIRTH AS ASSISTING ARTISTS	139
PROGRAM OF CONCERT WITH CELLIST DAVID POPPER	141
PROGRAM OF RECITAL BY EUGEN GURA	156

FOREWORD

By Helen Traubel

The title of Well-Tempered Accompanist, to which I heartily subscribe in principle, expresses, I must confess, an ideal state of artistic collaboration, rather than that frequently experienced over a period of years. For Bos, on occasion, can be unyielding as an "un-tempered accompanist" might well be—but with a well-tempered approach, he usually capitulates!

In reading the manuscript of "The Well-Tempered Accompanist," it occurred to me, in spite of the completeness of the treatment accorded various phases of the art of song, that the unique personal qualifications of Bos, as an accompanist and coach, his temperament and character, require a few words from one who has long been intimately associated with him.

From Bos' long experience with many great artists of the past, it is natural that his interpretive view should become somewhat fixed and standardized. While this is true, one of the points that has never ceased to surprise me, and one that has made possible an artistic collaboration lasting more than ten years, is that his approach to aesthetic problems has been one of flexibility which has taken into consideration special qualities of voice and understanding. Interpretations that were seemingly cast in fixed molds have been altered from time to time to permit of presentation to the public in a manner completely in conformity with inner convictions and vocal resources. This only serves to confirm what is implicit in the book: that tradition must not be a strait-jacket, but a living force, subject to change and growth.

This flexibility in the manner of approaching a song is also characteristic of Bos. In spite of his having been before the public continuously for fifty-four years, he retains a simplicity of nature which his oft-times cherubic countenance does not belie. The youthful freshness of his personal nature is one with the freshness of his artistic nature.

Although Bos' knowledge of voice is extensive and permits him to perceive the special qualifications and limitations of individual voices, in relation to song, with unusual keenness, he never encroaches upon the technical aspects of vocal production, which is the legitimate concern of trained vocalists and experienced instructors. Hence the chapter entitled "The Accompanist as Coach" should be of special interest and value to students of voice.

It is not to be thought that this volume will be of interest merely to accompanists, embryonic or otherwise. It should prove of unique value to everyone interested in the art of song, on both sides of the footlights as well as in the studio.

CHAPTER I

THE ACCOMPANIST'S BACKGROUND AND EQUIPMENT

The equipment of many accompanists of today is lacking in certain vital requirements: an intellectual background, an effortless technique, and an innate musical understanding. These are the basic essentials! Yet how they are neglected! It may be said that this neglect constitutes one of the more obvious errors in an educational system in which those with varying capacities have been trained as specialists according to their innate capabilities as well as accomplishments; but, all too frequently, with a false conception of the exacting requirements essential to the accompanist. This procedure has resulted in diverting many of lesser musicality and ability into the highly specialized and arduous field of accompanying. How often have mentors of musical aspirants remarked of those whose limited perception and technical insufficiency precluded careers as soloists: "Well, at least, they can become accompanists!" In this manner the greatest disservice is done music, as well as irreparable damage to the development and careers of students of music.

In an age when musical honors are frequently achieved overnight through a lucky Hollywood or radio "break," the long, hard road of the careful preparation of the accompanist is singularly lacking in allure to the musical aspirant. The requisites of craftsmanship in one of the most difficult phases of music are not often comprehended by the novitiate, and, if they are, lack attraction because they are devoid of the glamour generally associated with a musical career. "Success" is popularly seen as synonymous with "spot light"—and that is reserved for the soloists alone.

Yet, as we shall see, the artistic success of the soloist devolves in large measure upon the accompanist. It is upon him that the complete, balanced projection of the music depends. It is only through perfected collaboration of soloist and accompanist that a satisfying artistic entity may be attained. And the musical burden, if not the appeal of glamour, rests to a great extent upon the accompanist. In addition, the various, sometimes complex, facets comprising the artistic equipment of the professional accompanist must be counterbalanced by a personality capable of assuming a role in which self-abnegation plays an important part—even if a deceptive one. For, in appearance at least, the part of the accompanist is a modest one completely out of proportion to his weighty musical responsibilities and importance.

It is advisable to consider the intellectual background necessary to the proficient accompanist, inasmuch as this particular influence is seldom brought into focus or thoroughly understood. The art of the accompanist must of necessity presuppose an innately comprehending interest in poetry of different times and places reinforced by well-schooled knowledge of the structure of poetry and its musical investiture. This alone makes possible the appropriate synchronization of metrical and musical accents, and their delicate adjustment according to the demands of text and music. It is also necessary to the realization of the more subjective quality of "mood" and the varying emotional demands of texts intensified by music. From this indispensable knowledge, a sense of style, or rather of "styles," conditioned by the source of the texts and music as well as by the personalities of their creators, will be grasped and made capable of projection to auditors. While intuition is the "open Sesame" to such knowledge, it does not obviate trained and developed comprehension. This is the true educational process: "the intellectualization of the instinct."

Intelligent "interest in poetry of different times and places" demands a knowledge of languages. The general idea of poetry in translations is not sufficient. Phonetics of languages and the vocabulary of texts must be mastered in order to achieve that constantly maintained rapport with soloist, text, and music which is the primary, essential concomitant of the art of the accompanist. The achievement of his high goal necessitates, then, in addition to music education in all its aspects, courses in aesthetics, languages, and the the literature of the vocal repertoire as derived from various periods and peoples. Only in this way may an intuitive sense of style, essential as it is, be expanded into an authoritative comprehension of the stylistic textual demands of all periods.

The pianist who aspires to become an accompanist of superior attainment must have a technique of dependability and freedom. In fact, in order that he may be able to fulfill his manifold responsibilities in addition to playing the notes accurately, he must have reached the point technically in which "thought has passed from thinking." In other words, his technical equipment must have become second nature: completely devoid of effort or self-consciousness. It is only when this state is attained that the accompanist may be free to meet the more important demands upon his resourcefulness.

These "more important demands," in addition to constant awareness of the textual character of the composition at hand, involving, specifically, accents, nuances, phrases, rhetorical pauses, as well as all the structural demands inherent in both poetry and music, have largely to do with listening.

Every well-trained pianist is keenly aware of the value of listening. "Hear thyself!" is as important an injunction as "Know thyself!" But with the accompanist, the problem is more complex. Not only must he listen to himself, with his mind as well as with his inner ear, but he must be keenly alive to the tonal *quality* in addition to quantity in the performance of the soloist, whether vocalist or instrumentalist. Without such highly developed capacity to hear himself as well as the tone, either vocal or instrumental, of the soloist, the attainment of balance, which is quantitaitve, and the fusion of tone, which has to do with "quality" and is indissolubly linked with all superlative performances, are impossible of realization. To this end, another important aspect of the accompanist's special preparation comes into view:

Whether or not the accompanist has a voice of either quality or volume he must have studied singing sufficiently to have expert knowledge concerning the capabilities as well as limitations of the human voice. He must actually breathe and sing with the soloist, being careful that his vocal participation is inaudible, even in the first rows. If the accompanist is incapable of such rapport, a certain inflexibility will inevitably mar performances and make a perfect *ensemble* impossible of attainment.

In accompanying a singer, occasional compromises in phrasing are necessary, owing to the physical limitations of even the most highly developed voice. Similarly, a certain amount of knowledge must be acquired of instruments, their capabilities as well as limitations, if one is to be competent, in high artistic degree, to accompany such instruments as violin, 'cello, clarinet, etc. Naturally, complete mastery of all instruments is not possible, nor is it indispensable. Nevertheless, a practical, working knowledge of them must be had on the part of any accompanist who aspires to superlative attainment.

Two well-known compositions come to mind which illustrate the necessity for the accompanist's awareness of the limitations of the human voice and an instrument, but in which the musical values must not be sacrificed. The first of these is Schubert's *Lied*, entitled *Ganymede*. At the close of the song occurs this phrase which makes great demands upon the breath control of the singer:

Example 1

all - - lie-ben-der Va - - ter

Even though the vocalist has negotiated this difficult phrase successfully, without a *Luftpause*, Schubert requires that the phrase, in the following even more difficult version, be repeated:

Example 2

all — lie-ben-der Va — ter!

It may readily be perceived that in order to permit the singer to encompass the musical and vocal demands of these phrases without undue effort, or signs of loss of control and power, the accompanist must save the day. This may be done without compromise of artistic effect by an imperceptible increase in tempo. Such a hastening, if properly timed and adjusted, would be noted only by a metronome and never by the audience. If done obviously, a nervous conclusion to the song would be effected, even if the vocalist "saved face."

Such subtle and necessary adjustments in tempo which arise occasionally should be perceived by the accompanist whose duty it is to supply the quiet, constant current that carries the composition along naturally and inevitably, and not be left as a refuge to the soloist, who, occupying the spotlight, would immediately be revealed in unfavorable light to the auditors—not to mention the irreparable damage to the artistic value of the performance.

The second example illustrating the above points is Bach's well known Air, which appears on many violin programs as "Air for the G String." The opening of this requires the long sustaining of one note on the part of the soloist, to be accomplished on one continuous unbroken use of the bow. Many violinists are unable to meet this demand if the accompanist stolidly maintains a leisurely tempo. Here, again, an imperceptible forward urge to the tempo may be undertaken by the accompanist, without giving the impression that the soloist is a "thin-ice player" whose refuge is in speed. Nor will damage have been done the structure of the composition.

I recall an occasion, many years ago, on which I played this work with Albert Spalding for the first time. Having had experience with violinists who were unable to carry the opening tone on one bow if an undeviating, rigid tempo was preserved in the piano accompaniment, I gave a slight impetus to the tempo in order to make his task easier. Mr. Spalding stopped playing, put his hand on my shoulder, and said, comprehendingly: "When you play the opening of the Air with me, it will not be necessary to hasten the tempo." His mastery, musical and technical, was so great that such moments held no peril for him.

One exceedingly important aspect of the piano accompanist's special equipment is the technique of the damper pedal, frequently and incorrectly referred to as the "loud pedal." It might well be claimed that the very different application of the pedal in accompanying is more frequently misunderstood, even not grasped at all, than any other phase of the accompanist's highly specialized equipment.

Piano "color," attained through the release of overtones by pressing the right foot pedal, thus lifting the dampers from the strings, became the vogue with the composers and pianists of the 19th Century "Romantic" school. It has now become largely the fashion of pianists to use this highly enriched tonal medium in the performance of music of other than that of the so-called "romantic" period. While this is neither the time nor the place to go into the merits or demerits of such an indiscriminate procedure, it is most necessary to speak of the economy that should be practiced in the use of the pedal-enriched tone in accompanying.

Since it is the function of the accompanist to supply background and unobtrusive support to the soloist, as well as undercurrent to the whole, the injection of too lavish piano "color" through overpedalling inevitably results in upsetting that finely adjusted balance which must be sustained at all times. In other words, and more specifically, the pianist simply cannot allow himself to pedal in accompanying as he might be inclined to do, and more appropriately, when playing a solo.

The purpose of the "background" to be supplied by the accompanist might well be compared to the setting of a rare gem. The setting should not become so ornate or colorful that it obscures instead of intensifying the beauty of the jewel. Likewise, the pianist must restrain his fondness for color in order that the balance is not upset, and in order that the constantly maintained relation between the parts may result in the placement of all musical values in perspective.

Even in music where the use of pedal-enriched tone is appropriate and fitting, the accompanist must refrain from its lavish use. In fact, in certain compositions, such as Schubert's *Wohin?* and *Die Forelle* I abjure the use of pedal completely, playing very crisply, in order not to mar the delicate color which must be supplied by the singer. Similarly in serenades, where the accompanist simulates the plucking of strings in an informal manner, no pedal should be used. It is only too true that many pianists have recourse to constant use of pedal in order to obscure defects of touch. Hence the accompanist who would achieve the highest results must have a delicately adjusted, sensitive touch in which evenness and crispness may be maintained without subterfuge.

Even in the *Ständchen* by Richard Strauss and also that by Schubert, the skilled accompanist may refrain from pedal color. In the latter, the Schubert "Serenade," particular care should be taken to sustain the two-beat bass octaves their exact duration, playing the right hand in a light, plucked staccato. Then when the melodic, piano phrases occur, if they are played *molto legato,* the desired effect will have been achieved: one of most spontaneous simplicity. One must be artful in order to seem artless!

Also, the pianist who has been trained as a soloist must revise his conception of the use of the soft pedal in accompanying. The soloist reserves the use of the soft pedal for very special effects, being careful to refrain from its overuse. The accompanist, on the other hand, must have recourse more frequently to this mechanical aid in reducing tonal volume. There can be no set rules in the matter. The highly trained, sensitive ear alone must dictate the course to be followed, with eternal vigilance in maintaining balance inherent in the music and with due consideration for the tonal volume and color of the soloist's voice.

A less exacting but nonetheless important aspect of the accompanist's equipment must be a cultivated ability to read at sight, not only the two staves which every competent pianist should be able to encompass fluently, but, simultaneously, the additional staff of the soloist.

From this brief introduction to the art of the piano accompanist, it may readily be comprehended that the expert accompanist must have a knowledge of the whole similar to that which is possessed by a conductor, with these two essential differences: he must direct, *without seeming to direct,* and, in addition, he must play a dual role, one of pianism, and the equally important one of self-effacement.

But, unlike what many may think of him, the *Well-Tempered Accompanist* does not "lackey the heels of others."

CHAPTER II

THE SCHOOL OF EXPERIENCE

W<small>HILE</small> the formal education of the professional accompanist is indispensable to his adequate preparation, as I have endeavored to show in the introductory chapter, it is only in the school of experience that many essential elements of the art of accompanying are fully grasped.

My first professional engagement as an accompanist was with Raimund von Zur-Mühlen. I had proven to the satisfaction of this great singer that my pianistic and musical equipment were adequate, and that I could read music readily at sight. To test my ability in the latter respect, he placed several songs by Richard Strauss in front of me at the piano. After I had played them with ease, he remarked: "That is all that I wanted to see. You read at sight very satisfactorily. But I do not sing such trash. I sing only Schubert, Schumann, and Brahms." Von Zur-Mühlen excelled in singing the *Lieder* by these masters, but songs of Strauss and Hugo Wolf were too new and modern for his taste!

Having been engaged and complimented by this greatest *Lieder* singer of the day, and being only twenty years of age, I was very much puffed up and eager to show my mettle in public recital with him. The opportunity soon came, for von Zur-Mühlen had four recitals to give in the provinces near Berlin. We had adequate rehearsal, I was well prepared, and the press notices of my playing were good. I felt very much pleased with myself. But von Zur-Mühlen remained silent about my accompanying on the tour. After our return to Berlin, I said to him "I should like to have a few words with you." His pointed failure to mention my work, which I thought had been excellent, troubled me.

Von Zur-Mühlen replied: "I know what you wish to ask me. You want to know what I thought of your playing in our recitals. Your notices were good, but I have said nothing. That is because I thought your playing was terrible. You almost ruined my singing." Then he went on, saying that in one of the songs by Brahms I had failed to prepare his entrance by making a *crescendo,* as he had advised in rehearsal; that in one of the Schubert songs, similarly, I had forgotten to make an indicated *diminuendo.* In fact, so he said, I had spoiled his singing in these *Lieder.* He was furious. And I was equally chagrined. But I had learned an invaluable lesson, and one for which my completely adequate formal training had in nowise prepared me. For the first time I realized the necessity of studying the individual style of the soloist. It was not sufficient to know the musical demands of the score and to be adequate technically. There must be a complete understanding of the artistic personality of the singer and sympathy with it at all times, if perfect collaboration is to be attained. Otherwise, the soloist is placed at a disadvantage, and realization of his artistic conceptions rendered impossible.

My youthful conceit had received a severe jolt, but von Zur-Mühlen retained me as his accompanist, and I strove valiantly to live up to his exacting artistic demands. Still there was no word of commendation from him. Later we gave a recital in Berlin. After the recital I received a note from von Zur-Muhlen. He wrote: "Last night you must have played well, because I was not conscious of your playing throughout the recital." This was the first word of commendation, if such it can be termed, that I had received from my first taskmaster. My apprenticeship had been served. I had learned in the difficult and exacting school of experience.

But it was not until one year later that I was deemed worthy of von Zur-Mühlen's unqualified approval. It came, following a performance of the Schubert song cycle, *Die Schöne Müllerin*. Von Zur-Muhlen wrote: "At last I can tell you in good faith that you are now an accompanist without a peer. Last night your playing of Schubert's song cycle was completely in the musical style of the work, and, in addition, at all times you were in accord with my intentions." So, finally, I had reached the point where I had mistakenly thought I was when I had completed my formal musical training. In the school of experi-

Raimund von Zur-Mühlen

ence, however painful at times, I had not only learned something of the artistic requirements which are indispensable to the accompanist, I had also lost that unwarranted conceit which afflicts many young, inexperienced musicians. And satisfaction in true attainment is not to be confused with "conceit." At last I could look upon my artistic accomplishment and see "that it was good."

Other difficulties which I learned to surmount "the hard way," *i.e.*, in the school of experience, were the differences between accompanying instruments and voice. The instrumental musician in the professional field has, upon reaching maturity, many years of rigorous technical training and musical experience behind him. Consequently, the accompanist and the schooled instrumental musician have a common meeting ground derived from similar musical preparation. Conversely, people seldom discover that they have voices until they have reached the age of seventeen or eighteen. In many instances they have little or no musical background and the temptation to start a "career" on the strength of a beautiful voice, without awaiting a period of musical development which may only be achieved after many years of toil, is one to which many succumb. It might be said that one of the most unfortunate aspects of the singing profession is that frequently the artist who begins with primary dependence upon vocal opulence does not attain commensurate musical experience and knowledge until the vocal powers have begun to wane.

Marcella Sembrich

Fortunately, there are exceptions to this gloomy picture. There are many instances of musicians, after having had adequate vocational training in their profession, who discover upon reaching maturity that they have voices. One of the most notable examples of this was Marcella Sembrich. She had the advantage of being the daughter of a musician, and at the age of twelve played both violin and piano in public. She continued the study of these instruments for several years after making her public debut, before she "discovered" that she had a voice. Consequently, by the time her voice was thoroughly trained, she was a rare artist of high attainments, both vocally and musically. It is not difficult to perceive such artists. They loom on the artistic horizon.

While the accompanist may occasionally have the inspiring satisfaction of playing for singers whose musicianship equals their vocalism, there are many more disconcerting experiences to be had in accompanying those who are inadequately prepared musically. Under such circumstances, the accompanist must make a careful study of the singer's musical weaknesses, and endeavor to strengthen them so that they are not too obvious. As I learned through experience, there are many instances when faulty phrasing on the part of singers must be mitigated through corresponding flexibility in the accompaniment, at the same time retaining the continuity of the composition. Where the instrumentalist's conception of phrasing has been based entirely upon structural considerations, the singer, either through lack of musical knowledge or lack of breath, or both, may break the musical line. Such adjustments are learned only through practical experience. Since these deviations from organic musical procedure are unpredictable, and vary with different singers, the need of studying and completely understanding the idiosyncrasies of each singer becomes increasingly paramount.

If the singer is occasionally forced by shortage of breath to break a phrase the ultimate musical meaning of which is lost if the break of the musical line is not covered by the accompanist, it is essential, in this case, that the accompaniment proceed without such interruption. In fact, the flow of the music must not only be preserved but it must actually be intensified by the accompanist, if musical continuity is to be kept unbroken.

There are also many instances in songs, even by the greatest composers, in which the phrasing of words is counter to the musical phrasing. It is scarcely necessary to say that, in these cases, the phrasing becomes that of the words. This may seem contrary to the principles of good musicianship. Nevertheless, it is a necessary concession and one without which there would be no common meeting ground for singer and accompanist.

The matter of attaining proper balance through variations of tonal volume in accompanying instruments is easily solved by the pianist. Moments where the principal thematic material falls to the accompanist are brought out fully; similarly where one string instrument carries the main musical burden, or even two instruments as the case may be, the background of the piano must be sensitively adjusted so that at all times the necessary relationship between the parts, which constitutes musical perspective, is preserved. Such problems are solved through structural analysis and a delicate adjustment of tonal values. These are all predictable elements. They have to do with organic principles inherent in musical structure.

Although the same necessity for balance exists, naturally, in accompanying singers, here again unpredictable situations frequently arise which may not be perceived by the mere study of a musical score. One of these exigencies occurs most often owing to a lack of understanding very common to singers, that of the relative carrying quality of low tones when in close juxtaposition with higher ones. A good example of this may be comprehended in the following quotation from Schubert's *Aufenthalt*:

Whereas the musical accent comes on the beginnings of the words *Strom* and *Wald,* the singer is unaware that the next tone, an octave lower, both because of lack of musical emphasis and lack of height, easily becomes inaudible. The lower tone, so sharply contrasted with the one that immediately precedes it, may disappear without the singer's being aware of it. An instantaneous reduction of volume must be made on the lower tone by the accompanist also to obviate such a contingency.

Sensitivity to tonal inflections, so essential to that fusion which is the *sine qua non* of the expert accompanist, must, however, not be confined to such readily perceived, isolated musical moments. In a larger, more constant sense, the tone of the accompanist must ebb and flow, rise and fall, with the musical line. This constant, all-pervading element must enliven all musical conceptions and leaven the whole. Without this, the inner life of the music cannot be projected, whether in accompanying voice or instrument.

Another necessary adjustment that the accompanist must make occurs when words beginning with more than one consonant are sung. This is particularly true when the text is in German, as in Schubert's *Du Bist die Ruh.* At the words *voll Lust und Schmerz,* the alert singer who possesses a true sense of the richness of words will anticipate the consonants *sch* in the word *Schmerz,* occurring on the first beat, so that the accompaniment synchronizes his emphasis with the vowel "*e*," as:

[musical notation: "Ich wei-he dir___ voll Lust und Schmerz"]

Similarly, at the words *und schliesse du,* the accompanist must play with the diphthong *"ie,"* not with *sch* in the word *schliesse,* as:

[musical notation: "Kehr'ein bei mir, und schlie-se du"]

The peculiar richness of the German language in consonants imposes a special responsibility upon the accompanist who would become proficient in the playing of *Lieder*. However, corresponding instances arise in other languages, as with the word *tristesse* in French; and in English with the words *shreds, threads, snowy shrouds,* etc. Such instances are so numerous in all poetic texts set to music that the accompanist must be eternally vigilant in discovering and meeting them successfully himself.

A lesson in exact "timing" in the execution of arpeggiated, or "rolled" chords, I learned from Johannes Messchaert, whose accompanist I became after the retirement of von Zur-Mühlen. Messchaert was also one of the most notable singers of his day, and one from whom I learned many of the subtleties of the art of accompanying *Lieder*. In Schubert's *Meeres Stille* I found that the final tone of an arpeggiated chord must synchronize with the melodic tone. In other words the beat must be anticipated with the first tones of the "rolled" chord, the final tone of which should come on the beat, as:

This also occurs occasionally in accompanying instruments, and the example quoted herewith is the seldom performed arrangement of Bach's *Chaconne*, originally written for violin solo, by Robert Schumann, with the added piano accompaniment. The chords which open this work must be arpeggiated by the violinist, and the accompanist should take care that the accompanying chords coincide with the final tone of each chord, not with the first, as:

The art of the accompanist demands, above all, that he possess what is generally termed a "sympathetic" approach, both in a musical and personal sense. But it frequently happens that this very necessary quality degenerates into sloppiness and sentimentality in performance. This is especially to be perceived when accompanists, in a mistaken effort to infuse their playing with the aforementioned "sympathy," indulge in the unforgivable musical sin of anticipating the right hand with the left, when the "attack" should be simultaneous in both hands. This inexcusable fault is not merely confined to the dilettante, but sometimes unwittingly creeps into the playing of the professional accompanist. It is as though the left hand were saying to the right hand, apologetically, in the famed style of Mrs. Malaprop: "Do you precede me and I will go before!"

After a recital in Berlin, early in my career, Lessmann, the great German music critic, came to see me and said: "You play such admirable accompaniments that it is too bad that your peformance is sometimes marred by a lack of coordination of the hands." Quite unconsciously I had evidently fallen into the faulty mannerism I am now warning against. I was very grateful for advice from a critic who was kind enough to give me a needed lesson privately instead of in the public press. After that, I watched myself carefully, and made the correction without difficulty. I also had the reward of warm commendation from Lessmann in his review of my next recital.

Although the accompanist may be meticulous in all the technical details and musical subleties necessary to expert performance, his art unenlivened by imagination will never reach the heights of true artistry. This need was forcefully brought home to me in my early association with such masters of the art of singing as von Zur-Mühlen and Messchaert. One episode occurred with von Zur-Mühlen which opened up new vistas to my musical imagination. I was rehearsing Tosti's song *Ridonami la Calma,* and had played the four half note opening chords just as they were written, expecting von Zur-Mühlen to begin singing. But he stopped me and reproached me sternly: "Have you no imagination—no understanding of what this song is about? I am to sing a prayer. You play four chords as if all you had to do was to give me the key in which I am to sing. The first chord must be the loud clang of a bell, as you approach a church. As you enter the church, the ringing of the bell becomes gradually less loud, until, with the fourth and final chord of the introduction, played very softly, you have put me in a prayerful mood."

Such was the lesson I have never forgotten, and it made me realize that even though one possesses all of the catalogued attributes of the proficient accompanist, without imagination his playing will merely be "a sounding brass and tinkling cymbal."

CHAPTER III

SUITING THE ACTION TO THE WORD

The art of accompanying *Lieder* poses many special problems, requiring not only superlative qualities of musicianship and intimate knowledge of poetry, but, in many instances, acquaintance with the writing habits and idiosyncrasies of their composers.

This is particularly true in the case of Franz Schubert, whose unparalleled creative activity resulted in the production of more than 600 songs, many of which were incomparable masterpieces. However, the creation of so vast a number of songs, together with a colossal output in other forms of composition, precluded their revision by a composer whose span of life was fated to be very short. Their first, sometimes very informal, draft was all the attention given them, although a superabundance of genius was lavished upon them at the moment of creation. From the terrific energy and haste of Schubert in composition developed a very common habit of writing the melody and accompaniment once only, although the poem might have several verses. This was a simplification which publishers, however, seldom permitted to stand.

Consequently, we have many examples of Schubert's songs, as published, appearing with the identical music which was written and marked by him for the initial verse only, repeated several times without change of markings, although the moods and meanings of the several verses may differ. To follow such a procedure is most certainly contrary to Schubert's intention as well as esthetically false, and makes of many of his works what might be called "*da capo* music," that is, music which is merely repeated mechanically without variation in markings.

Many examples of this may be found in Schubert's songs, but it will suffice to mention only a couple of them here: the three-verse *Auf dem Wasser zu singen,* and *Das Wandern,* the opening song of the cycle *Die Schöne Müllerin.* In the case of *Das Wandern* the publisher has used the melody and accompaniment once only, but has permitted all five verses of Wilhelm Müller's poem to appear, the musical markings being unchanged from those indicated by Schubert for the first verse. A literal rendition, without variation and due regard for the inherent, different character of each verse, could only result in such textual monotony that their essential meanings would be lost and the whole imbued, in addition, with an insufferable sameness. So stifling an adherence to the "letter" can only result in a quenching of that revealing spirit which must quicken the approach to any work of art. By studying the various meanings of the five verses, the informed accompanist will soon discover for himself the different moods, and be guided accordingly. The appropriate markings, which should change according to the mood of the moment, should not be reduced to formula. However, I may indicate my conception of the several tonal volumes of the accompaniment of *Das Wandern* as follows: 1st Verse: *mezzo forte;* 2nd Verse: *pianissimo;* 3rd Verse: *mezzo forte;* 4th Verse: *fortissimo;* 5th and closing Verse: *forte* with enthusiasm. Needless to say, if the singer and accompanist do not see "eye to eye" on the dynamics and expression, the result will be most unfortunate!

I may say that the most discerning eye and ear may not discover all of the pitfalls into which the careless accompanist (not to mention singer) may easily fall. Errors in musical rendition which frequently grow from tradition rooted in ignorance and false esthetic values are not always so flagrant and obvious as those I have mentioned.

Even the composer himself is sometimes remiss in the treatment of textual subleties with the result that the full value of these is not realized. Such an instance was pointed out to me by von Zur-Mühlen in Schumann's ecstatic, noble love song, *Widmung*. Schumann, in his musical setting of the text, wrote, in the middle section of the song:

> "*Du bist die Ruh
> Du bist der Frieden,
> Du bist vom Himmel
> Mir beschieden.*"

When von Zur-Mühlen sang this song to Clara Schumann's accompaniment, she pointed out that the fourth line should not read *"vom Himmel,"* but "der Himmel," in accordance with the original text of Rückert's poem. It may readily be discerned that "Thou art *the* heaven given to me," together with the similar treatment accorded the attributes of "Rest" and "Peace," in *"Ruh"* and *"Frieden,"* is much stronger than the sentiment implicit in *"vom Himmel,"* or *"from* heaven." Yet such is the power of custom that frequently when singers have made this correction upon my advice, based upon proper authority, it has been questioned by those whose conception has derived from an error perpetuated by the publishers of Schumann's masterpiece.

The mention of Clara Schumann's name always evokes happy memories of this remarkable woman, whom I met only once and with whom I had hoped to study had not fate decreed otherwise. But this one meeting has always held such significance for me that it brings us to one of the most interesting episodes as well as far-reaching influences in my life.

My teacher at the Amsterdam Conservatory, from which I was graduated in 1895, was Julius Röntgen, eminent composer, pianist, teacher, and conductor; later director of the Conservatory. Röntgen, among his other outstanding talents, was famous for his accompanying, particularly of *Lieder,* and his recitals with Johannes Messchaert, widely known as the Messchaert-Röntgen *Lieder* evenings, were among the important musical events of the day. Having long been an intimate friend of Clara Schumann who had been interested in his unusual abilities since childhood, Röntgen was eager for me to have the advantage of study with the widow of one of Germany's greatest composers, little realizing that "one of the greatest pianoforte players the world has ever heard" was so close to the end of her long and distinguished career. So in the summer of 1895, Röntgen arranged an audition for me. I played for her and was overjoyed to be accepted as her pupil. Unfortunately for me, Madame Schumann's death occurred in the spring of the following year before I could realize my ambition for study, but my one brief interview with this unforgettable woman and artist colored my musical conceptions throughout my entire career. For Clara Schumann's devotion to and unique understanding of her husband's works was manifested with great insight and graphic power on this occasion, so momentous for me. From my playing of one of Schumann's *Lieder* a discussion of the extended closing section, a peculiar and highly individual characteristic of his genius, arose. Madame Schumann told me that, in many instances, Schumann's markings for postludes were idealistically conceived by him, and while these might be appropriate if one were playing the songs for one's own enjoyment, or in a small room for a few friends, they would prove anti-climactic in public performance, and, consequently, should be ignored.

Now in my studies at the Conservatory I had been taught to regard every dynamic marking of the composer as sacrosanct. But Madame Schumann, whose regard for the spirit of her husband's works transcended mere adherence to the letter, explained that in such a song as *Frühlingsnacht,* in which the singer ends ecstatically, a *diminuendo* should not be made, as marked at the end, but, rather, the mood should be sustained by the accompanist throughout the piano postlude, until the final close. Otherwise, she explained, the song would fail in its effect upon an audience, and its total artistic result be weakened. Of course, this consummate artist was speaking from the depths of long, practical experience gained in public performance—not merely from an "ideal," theoretical point of view. Nor was her attitude actuated by interest in specious or sensational effect, but derived from the deepest love and highest artistic aims.

Many *Lieder* in which similar changes in the markings indicated by composers should be made are *Widmung* by Schumann, *Meine Liebe ist Grün* by Brahms, and also Brahms' *Minnelied*. In fact, in the last two songs mentioned, the intensity of both words and music, attaining a cumulative height in the final phrases performed by the singer, should be continued by the accompanist with ever greater intensification to the very end of the piano postlude. In other words, the final mood of the singer should be maintained in the accompanist's closing phrases, if the complete, inherent possibilities of text and music are to be realized, and their innermost meaning projected to the glory of the music and the edification of auditors.

Thus, through the illuminating words of Clara Schumann I was inducted into the mystery of the appropriate treatment of the postludes to *Lieder,* which attained a special significance with Schumann. However, I realized with great clarity and conviction that it only become a "mystery" if the underlying esthetic principle were not completely comprehended. As in all such experiences as the one related above, it is the opening up of new and hitherto unforeseen vistas which make possible the continuance of one's artistic development and the attainment of heights which may only be scaled through imaginative flights. The new vista opened up to me revealed the underlying principle in clear perspective, being merely the natural, appropriate treatment expounded in Hamlet's famous instruction to the players: "Suit the action to the word; the word to the action."

The following year, I had an experience which confirmed even more forcefully what I had learned in principal from Clara Schumann. Brahms had just completed that work which proved to be his last published composition, *Vier Ernste Gesänge.* The songs were written for Anton Sistermans whose baritone voice was ideally suited to their rendition, and I had the honor and privilege of accompanying their first performance in Vienna in the spring of 1896. Brahms himself was present for this great occasion and the audience, large and distinguished, acclaimed both composer and performers. At the conclusion of the concert Brahms came to the artists' room and warmly thanked both Sistermans and myself for our performances which had, so he said, perfectly realized his intentions. In fact, Sistermans had so carefully observed Brahms' markings that the four songs, based upon Biblical text, emerged to their final close as an unbroken series of philosophical meditations, whether they dealt with reflections that death is better than life, from Ecclesiastes, or St. Paul's conclusion that love is the greatest of all things.

Although Brahms had written *Vier Ernste Gesänge* for Sisterman's low voice, I was engaged two weeks later to play them for von Zur-Mühlen, transposed into a higher key. During rehearsal von Zur-Mühlen told me that he could not sing the final phrases of St. Paul's words, the famous definition of love, taken from the First Epistle to the Corinthians, as Brahms had marked them: *diminuendo* and *piano*. He felt that the words *die Liebe ist die Grösseste unter ihnen,* which are repeated by Brahms, demanded an effect of cumulative power—not of anti-climactic reflection. It was as if in tones of the utmost finality he was proclaiming that "this is all ye know on earth and all ye need to know." So he instructed me: "When you approach the ending of the fourth song, not only make an intensification of tone at the reiteration of the words *die Liebe ist die Grösseste unter ihnen,* but continue the *crescendo* after I have finished singing, to the close of the piano postlude, ending triple *forte*."

Again Brahms was present for the public performance, and the acclaim was even greater than at the original performance. And again Brahms came to the artist's room and had only the warmest praise for the magnificent rendition of his songs. Afterwards, von Zur-Mühlen said to Brahms: "Master, I hope you are not furious with me for ending your Biblical songs with a great climax."

Brahms replied: "You sang them magnificently. I did not notice anything wrong."

It is evident that Brahms, as he approached the close of his life, was able to reflect with equal detachment upon "life," "death," and "love." But to von Zur-Mühlen, that which emerged as the sum total of all things, after the philosophical detachment inherent in the first three songs of the *Vier Ernste Gesänge,* demanded a glowing, passionate climax. And this conception had been justified in performance, even to Brahms' satisfaction.

Many times, subsequently, I had occasion to recall the early experiences with Brahms' final masterworks. One of these later episodes occurred in Vienna in 1937 when I was on tour with the American singer, Rose Bampton. We were staying in the Bristol Hotel. One day, as I was passing through the lobby, Paul Stefan, the well-known Viennese music critic, was interviewing Miss Bampton. Stefan recognized me, and, recalling that first performance of the *Vier Ernste Gesänge* in 1896, when Brahms was in the audience, engaged me in a lengthy conversation. What was scheduled to be an interview with Miss Bampton developed into a discussion of my early experiences. The next day an article by Paul Stefan appeared in the newspaper *Die Stunde*. It recounted most graphically the story of my performances with Sistermans and von Zur-Mühlen as related above.

Stefan's article created quite a sensation, and the evening of Miss Bampton's recital I was visited by many curious people in the "green room" who were eager to talk with the one who had played for Brahms on an historic occasion and had been commended by the great master. Such is fame and the power of reflected glory!

Incidentally, at my suggestion, Miss Bampton sang a song by Schubert which was unknown to the Viennese public that prided itself upon familiarity with the works of one of its most illustrious sons, namely *Der Fluss*. This work is to be found only in the complete collection of Schubert's songs published by Breitkopf and Härtel. It has never ceased to be a mystery to me that singers persist in adhering to the public performance of such a limited number of Schubert's numerous masterpieces of *Lieder,* when an adventurous spirit and appropriate research would bring to light many unfamiliar creations of his genius, thereby enriching the vocal repertoire.

The most memorable performances of Brahms' great Biblical songs were those by Ludwig Wüllner, whose accompanist I was for many years. Although Wüllner's voice was not an example of that *bel canto* which characterized the art of von Zur-Muhlen, Messchaert, Sembrich, Julia Culp, and many others whom I accompanied later, his expressive resources and dramatic power were unequalled. His ability to evoke the profoundest meanings of both text and music was such that even those who at first questioned his lack of vocal finish eventually came under the spell of his consummate art. So, in retrospect, those performances of Brahms' *Vier Ernste Gesänge* which loom most vividly on the musical horizon of memory are those by Ludwig Wüllner. Their spiritual atmosphere was so all-pervading that even when he sang them in the ugly hall of the Gebouw van Kunsten en Wetenschappen at the Hague in Holland, the huge stage and generally unsightly hall seemed to me to be transformed into a vast cathedral in which the towering climax of *die Liebe ist die grösseste unter ihen* seemed a final consummation which indeed became "all ye know on earth, and all ye need to know."

CHAPTER IV

TRADITIONS IN THE MAKING

AFTER graduation from the Amsterdam Conservatory in 1895, I went to Berlin during the summer to do some additional studying and await an opportunity to pursue my chosen career of accompanist. The opportunity came soon.

Max Friedländer, the eminent authority on the German *Lied*, was giving a series of lectures at the University of Berlin. Quite by chance I dropped in to hear one of his classes, arriving somewhat late. It seems that, prior to my arrival, Friedländer had asked for volunteers from the audience to illustrate some points he had made, asking specifically if anyone present played Beethoven's "Waldstein" Sonata. A friend with whom I was sitting, knowing that I was equipped to supply the desired illustrations, urged me to go forward and offer my services. However, since I had not heard all of the lecture, I was not disposed to risk the "limelight."

At the close of Friedländer's lecture, my friend took me to meet him, and what seemed at first to be merely a chance acquaintance grew into my first invaluable experience in that which might aptly be termed "the creation of an artistic tradition." For, at that time, Friedländer had undertaken the collection and editing of Schubert's songs for the Peters Edition, and required a pianist who could assist him in this colossal task.

He asked me to visit him, and, after testing my ability to read and transpose music at sight, I was engaged as his assistant in the revision of the now famous Peters Edition of Schubert's *Lieder.* For the balance of that year, I went every morning to his studio, transposing songs written for one voice into lower or higher keys, as the case might be, checking for inaccuracies, and, above all, comparing the available printed copies with Schubert's originals for discrepancies in text or music. For my two hours' daily work Friedländer paid me the enormous sum of fifty *pfennige* per hour, or the equivalent of little more than ten cents! But what knowledge I derived from this rigorous training I have used profitably all of my life. It might even be said properly that my artistic gain was in inverse ratio to the financial emolument.

Friedländer had also been engaged to make a collection of the various musical settings of Goethe's poems by the contemporaries of the great German poet. This was a very exacting project, entailing much research, editing, and, at least in one instance, the writing of the piano accompaniment. Although Friedländer took credit for the work, which eventually became the 11th volume of the *Schriften der Goethe-Gesellschaft,* in actuality I did practically all of the labor in connection with this interesting undertaking. He even failed to mention my name in giving credit to those who contributed to the project, although others whose concern was relatively insignificant were duly mentioned in the "Foreword."

Most of the settings of the Goethe poems are practically unknown today. But it was an interesting comparative study to place side by side musical settings of Goethe's *Erlkönig* by Reichardt, Klein, Zelter, Corona Schröter, Schubert, and Löwe. Similarly *Das Veilchen*, usually associated with Mozart, was also set to music by three other composers of Goethe's day; *Mignon*, by four composers, including Beethoven and Spontini; *Heidenröslein*, also by four composers, of whom Schubert's setting is best known; *An den Mond*, by five composers, including Schubert; and so on. The piano accompaniment of *Das Veilchen*, composed by Herzogin Anna Amalia for string quartet and winds, was my arrangement. Although time has eliminated most of these various musical settings of Goethe's great poems and even memory of many of the composers of that period, this research has afforded me invaluable insight and experience in relative musical values.

In addition to the work of assisting him in the editing of Schubert's masterpieces and research into musical settings of Goethe's texts, Friedländer also engaged me to illustrate his weekly lectures at the University of Berlin, for which he paid me ten marks, about $2.50, per session. In these lectures I widened the scope of acquaintance with other song literature, from *Lieder* by Beethoven to ballads of Löwe. Friedländer's vast knowledge of song was derived not only from profound musicianship and wide research, but from his practical experience as a singer, gained from study with Manuel Garcia in London and Julius Stockhausen in Frankfurt, as well as from extensive public singing. It will undoubtedly be recalled by many that he later became an exchange professor at Harvard and made a lecture tour of America, including twenty universities.

My apprenticeship with Friedländer had a very happy result. He was sufficiently pleased with my work to introduce me to the great singer Eugen Gura, who, although he had retired from the operatic stage, was widely acclaimed as one of the foremost *Lieder* singers of the day. He was particularly an authority in songs of Schubert, and my fresh experiences with Friedländer served me well at this juncture. For, as a result of Friedländer's recommendation, Gura engaged me for my first concert tour, as well as what proved to be his last. The first recital took place in Greifswald, March 9, 1896, followed by one in Stralsund, March 12. Audience and press reaction were favorable. In fact, my spurs had been won, and Gura engaged me for his 100th and final recital in Berlin, which took place in the great hall of the Philharmonie, April 11, 1896. The house was sold out. My fee for this concert was 40 marks, or about $10.00! I was now a full-fledged professional accompanist, although my artistic life was only at its inception—a fact I would certainly not have believed if anyone had told me so at that time.

My early experiences with Friedländer and Gura in the Schubert tradition were followed with unique opportunities to obtain accurate and intimate knowledge of the essential character and styles of other masters of song composition.

From von Zur-Mühlen, of whose influence upon my accompanying I have spoken in the chapter entitled *The School of Experience*, I gained authentic and authoritative perception into the songs of Schumann. Von Zur-Mühlen, long associated with Clara Schumann, with whom he gave many successful recitals of her husband's songs, was justly considered the leading exponent of these deeply conceived, stylistically difficult masterpieces.

In the year 1901 began an association which I may truly say had the most far-reaching effect upon my artistic life. I became accompanist to Ludwig Wüllner, and we toured extensively in Europe and America from that time until his final recital in Berlin in 1938. Wüllner's background was so unusual that it should be spoken of here in order that a clear idea may be obtained of the great artistic personality into which he developed.

Wüllner's father, Franz, as pianist, conductor, and composer, had held some of the most important musical posts in Germany for many years. In these various capacities he was intimately associated with

Dr. Ludwig Wüllner and Coenraad V. Bos

the leading creative musicians of the day. Although raised in and profoundly influenced by an intensely musical atmosphere, Ludwig was not at first trained to become a professional musician, least of all a singer, but studied philology and German literature at Munich, Berlin and Strassburg. After taking his Doctor's degree he taught German Literature at the Münster Academy for a short time, later becoming a dramatic actor. He had, also, the advantage of study at the Cologne Conservatorium, before going on the stage at Meiningen in 1889.

Wüllner became a favorite of the Grand Duke of Meiningen, and regular musical events of court life were the Sunday evening concerts at which he, accompanied by Johannes Brahms, sang *Lieder* by the master. Brahms came to consider Wüllner as the ideal interpreter of his songs, and it was through the composer's urgent advice that the dramatic actor became a concert singer.

From Wüllner I came to have a new insight into the innermost meanings of musical texts. His musical knowledge was commensurate with his profound grasp of literature, but the aspect of vocalization, of *bel canto*, as a means towards an end, did not appeal to him. The recreative process, as conceived by Wüllner, was, rather, similar to that of the original creator of a song—the musical investiture of poetry. The approach of the trained vocalist, to display a beautiful organ, was foreign to his nature and background. At first, this seemed strange to many people, especially to a master of song such as von Zur-Mühlen, but as they became better acquainted with the true depth and sincerity of Wüllner's art, they became his most ardent admirers.

From Wüllner I derived a new respect for the text, and phrasing became essentially linked with the words, rather than with the music This was especially true of the Brahms *Lieder*, many of which he had sung with the composer for the first time, and from whom he had received first-hand counsel for their appropriate rendition. To this day, it never fails to shock me when I hear some *Lieder* singers break the textual line of a song such as Brahms' *Mainacht*, in order to gain time and breath for a prolonged passage. Wüllner, in spite of vocal limitations, never permitted such a deviation from just artistic procedure. And, in all my artistic life, I have never accompanied a singer capable in the same degree of the projection of dramatic power and intensity of expression emanating from both words and music.

Although Hugo Wolf's creative life had come to a close with his incarceration in an asylum before my professional career brought me in contact with his works, in 1903 Wüllner and I were in Stuttgart and had the benefit of advice from Otto Faisst, who, although only an amateur, had been one of Wolf's closest friends. From Faisst's intimate knowledge of the composer and his songs, and later from the pianist Dr. Heinrich Potpeschnigg in Vienna, I received much important information concerning Wolf's

Helen Traubel and Coenraad V. Bos

Postcard from Richard Strauss

compositions and the stylistically appropriate manner of their rendition which subsequently I was able to put to very good use, thereby increasing the value and effectiveness of their presentation.

In Wolf's *Gesang Weyla's* I had been puzzled by the word *Orplid* in the line *Du Bist Orplid mein Land*. It is not surprising, then, to find that although many singers perform this song, they do so without knowing the meaning of this mysterious word. Faisst told me that the young poet Mörike, while walking in the country with his friend Streicher, had a poetic conception of an ideal land of his dreams which was nameless. For the purposes of the poem, Mörike and Streicher devised the word *Orplid* which seemed to the young men to portray their dream-land most euphoniously—hence its use in the text of one of Wolf's best known songs.

My first extensive experiences with the songs of Richard Strauss came from accompanying Strauss' wife, Pauline de Ahna, an artist of distinction, if not the possessor of an extraordinary voice. Strauss was frequently present at rehearsals and offered suggestions. One of these, involving a rather drastic change in Strauss' *Ständchen*, has, curiously enough, never been incorporated in the published editions. Strauss indicated that at the high note in the climax of the song, the singer should sustain the tone longer than written, and that the accompanist should at the same time repeat the accompanying piano figuration to support the singer, as:

I once asked Strauss why he did not indicate this change so that his wishes would be known and could be easily followed by everyone who sang or played his *Ständchen*. He merely shrugged his shoulders and said: "Why go to the trouble?"

Strauss was especially pleased with my playing of his song *Morgen*, that particularly beautiful work in which the pianist carries the principal melody in the accompaniment, while the singer intones an *obbligato* part. He once remarked that no one played the closing phrases, with their deeply reflective pauses, indicated by rests, as effectively as I did. As a matter of fact, I was always very careful to count the pauses out, silently of course, so that their full significance and the subsiding emotion of the song would be completely realized.

When Strauss was brought to America by the Brunswick Company for orchestral concerts and recitals of his works, with the composer conducting and accompanying, a series of four Town Hall song recitals in New York was arranged. The singers selected for these important events were Elisabeth Schumann, Claire Dux, Elena Gerhardt and George Meader. Although I prepared Mr. Meader for his program, Strauss accompanied all four recitals.

When Strauss felt like accompanying, he was the ideal performer of his own works. Consequently I looked forward to these historic recitals with the keenest anticipation. The orchestral programs in Carnegie Hall were enormously successful. The houses were sold out and the reception from the public and press was all that could have been wished. But for some inexplicable reason, the song recitals were rather poorly attended, considering their significance, the auditorium being only half filled for each occasion. The effect upon Strauss was disastrous. His interest in playing flagged to such a degree that when he came to *Morgen* the eloquent pauses at the close, upon which he placed such stress, were completely ignored! I am sure no one was more astonished than I was.

Richard Strauss was famous for the sharpness of his tongue. An amusing instance of this occurred at a banquet in Vienna. Julia Culp was present, sitting opposite him at the table. Culp, a consummate artist, had for years sung only two of Strauss' songs in her public recitals, namely *Morgen* and *Heimliche Aufforderung*. Strauss, with enormous sarcasm, said to her: "Julia, do you still sing my *two* songs?" To which Madame Culp promptly replied, with equal emphasis: "I shall sing more of your songs *when you learn how to write for the human voice*."

As Julia Culp's accompanist over a period of years, I was well aware of her vocal limitations, which were not generally apparent to the public because of her unusual knowledge concerning her own capabilities and their limits. As a matter of fact, her range was in all probability less than that of any singer who attained similar artistic stature, extending, as it did, slightly more than an octave and one half, from middle C to second G flat. But such was the perfection of the tones within this relatively small range, and such was her extraordinary ability to imbue them with emotional color and dynamic variety, that she frequently gave the impression of possessing no limitations of range. In such songs as Schubert's *Du bist die Ruh*, in which she sang intervals extending from middle C to the second F above, the effect was one of such tonal opulence and emotional intensity that the range

Julia Culp

seemed much greater than it actually was. The secret of this great singer's consummate art truly lay in the fact that she had mastered the meaning of the ancient injunction: *Know Thyself!* As a consequence, she never permitted any weaknesses to become apparent to the public.

Much of my professional life occurred during a time in which many of the great *Lieder* were being introduced for the first time to the world and I was by force of circumstances in an environment in which traditions were in the making. In addition, I always made it my business to take advantage of every opportunity that afforded first-hand knowledge or contact with the originators of the great *Lieder* traditions. It is as much owing to this eagerness to go to original sources as it is to chance, luck, or fate, as it is variously called, that my experiences as an accompanist have been so rich and varied. "Tradition" for the accompanist, as for any other musician, must be a living thing in which one participates creatively.

CHAPTER V

BEGINNINGS, ENDINGS, AND
VARIOUS AD INTERIM PROBLEMS

It has always been the custom for accompanists to close the lid of the grand piano when playing for singers. This has arisen from the fact that most singers regard the emergence of the piano tone to a degree commensurate with that of the soloist as an encroachment upon their prerogatives. Also, it is undoubtedly true that most accompanists are incapable of adjusting properly the tonal balance between instrument and voice with the lid of the piano raised. Consequently, I have adhered, until recently, to the usual procedure of having the lid closed when playing for singers, only permitting the forward part open to allow the music rack to be in place. However, for purposes of appropriate balance, the small stick of the grand piano should be used when playing chamber music; and for dramatic recitations, formerly more in vogue than at the present time, such as Max von Schilling's *Hexenlied* and Richard Strauss' *Enoch Arden*, the lid should be completely raised to attain the desired strength of volume.

An experience in California, on tour with the

great dramatic soprano, Helen Traubel, led to a productive series of experiments with the lid of the piano from which many accompanists as well as singers might well profit. We were in the midst of a recital at Stanford University, in Palo Alto, when a note from Dr. Warren D. Allen, then head of the music department of the university and well-known writer on music, was received. It asserted that the piano was furnishing insufficient tone to support the great volume of Traubel's voice, and suggested raising the lid for the balance of the recital. Madame Traubel agreed to the suggestion, although we had never before attempted such an arrangement—and with astonishing result. I was, of course, careful to modulate my tone when necessary, so as not to overbalance the vocal tone in quieter passages, nor to overpower in the louder. But the effect upon Traubel was what was most surprising. Standing in the embrasure of the piano, with the lid raised behind her, she became aware of a new freedom in projecting her tones into the large auditorium. The lid of the piano furnished a natural resonator which deflected the tone without loss from the stage to the audience!

After this chance occurrence, we repeated the experiment in Seattle, Washington, with the same beneficial results, and now it is the established procedure when I accompany Helen Traubel. Not many singers, however, are willing to try so revolutionary an experiment, not only because few possess the volume and wide dynamic range of Traubel, but for other reasons not difficult to imagine. The delicate adjustments which must be maintained at all times between accompanist and singer are by no means confined to tonal considerations!

Much devolves upon the accompanist which is not to be found on the printed page of music! It is largely owing to lack of such indicated directions that some of the finest examples of song literature are seldom to be found on recital programs. The outstanding case of this is, I believe, the composer Robert Franz, whose songs have practically disappeared from the concert hall, although they include some of the most poetic and inspired *Lieder* ever written. Franz' songs, for the greater part, are disarmingly simple, unpretentious creations of great lyrical beauty. However, their seeming simplicity is very deceptive. Unlike Schumann, who delighted in piano postludes, and appropriate introductory, instrumental phrases, Franz usually dispenses entirely with the introduction, and seldom has any postlude whatever. In fact, the singer is frequently called upon to begin the song before the piano is heard. This peculiar and extreme reticence on the part of the composer imposes a responsibility upon singers which few are able to meet, and which none should be called upon to face unassisted by the accompanist—in spite of the complete lack of help from the composer.

For example, take Robert Franz' dark and tragic song of autumn, *Im Herbst*. If performed in the original key of C minor, the singer is called upon to sing the opening tone, G, without accompaniment, the piano entering with the second word *Heide* as:

Die Hei-de ist braun, einst blüh-te sie rot;___ die

Although some singers fortunately possess the gift of absolute pitch, and would be able to begin the song unassisted, such responsibility before an audience tends to place the soloist under undue strain. I found a simple and effective solution to the problem in very softly and unobtrusively arpeggiating, or rolling, the chord of the opening key, in this case C minor, begining in the bass and repeating twice, each time an octave higher. However, the highest tone of this unscheduled introduction must, as I learned from experience, be the interval of the singer's opening, in this case the fifth of the scale, G, taking particular care not to play the right hand of the chord, in the extent of an octave, in its fundamental position as this would make the upper tone C. Under similar circumstances, I once played a preliminary chord when accompanying Elena Gerhardt, and she began the song in the right key but on the wrong interval. I never took such a chance again!

Although the familiar, old saying has it that "all's well that ends well," the adage does not hold true in musical performance. Rather, it is the beginning and the ending which must be flawlessly executed, and slight deviations in between, should they occur, may be forgotten, or, at least, forgiven! As the songs of Robert Franz present a peculiar difficulty to the singer in the opening phrases, so they pose another problem at their final notes. And, again, the accompanist must be aware of the difficulty, and prepared, both psychologically and physically, to cope with a responsibility which is as much his as the singer's. Here again Franz' *Im Herbst* serves admirably to illustrate the point.

At the close of this song, as so frequently the case with Franz' *Lieder*, there is no piano postlude, the singer and accompanist ending with a *ritenuto* simultaneously. Although the final tone, on the word *todt,* is not marked with a hold, it should be sustained at length by the singer, the vowel "o" being elongated. At the same time the accompanist must be careful not to release the final chord before the singer has finished. In this case, as well as in similar ones, I carefully watch the soloist, and do not release the concluding notes until the singer has closed the elongated vowel of the word *todt* with the final consonant "t." Any final impression of an abrupt conclusion under such circumstances, on the part of either singer or accompanist, would inevitably lead to an embarrassing silence. And it is during such an unfortunate silence that the whole rendition of the song, no matter how pronounced its many virtues might have been, fails in the sustaining of mood. Its complete artistic result is consequently lost and that all-important element of conviction, without which an audience is never deeply moved, dissipated into thin air.

There are other instances in song literature in which beginnings are similarly unadorned by composers but which are not coped with so simply and easily by the accompanist. Such an example comes to mind in Hugo Wolf's *Elfenlied*. In this case, also, the singer begins without the indicated support of accompanying tones on the part of the composer. Moreover, the singer's initial tone is not an interval of the first chord of the song's opening key, but the 7th degree, or leading tone, D, of the key of E-flat. The singer should, therefore, be given a cue by rolling the chord of the dominant 7th, with the upper tone D, as follows, leading in the manner of the song's beginning into E-flat:

A still more difficult beginning for the singer is posed by Jensen's *Weisst du noch?* Starting, without piano accompaniment, in the key of B-flat, the singer is called upon to execute the interval of the major 7th, or A, above a tonic six-four chord in the accompaniment. This dissonant opening must be more elaborately prepared by the accompanist, and I have found it advisable, if one does not wish to invite disaster, nonchalantly to improvise an introduction by harmonizing and playing the opening three note motive, A,G,D, in the manner of the song, thus:

Here it will be noted that I did not resolve the final chord of the improvised introduction, making it more imperative that the singer enter with the natural sequence of the song.

In the foregoing examples and suggestions for preparing the singer to cope easily with the beginnings of songs to which composers have not given formal introductions, it must be well understood that under no circumstances should the accompanist convey the impression to the audience that the songs under discussion, as well as innumerable similar compositions, possess introductions which are integral parts of the songs. Neither should it appear that the accompanying pianist is supplying something the composer neglected to write down. The only valid use of such seemingly spontaneous and entirely uncalculated cues to the singer lies in their unobtrusive, improvisatorial character. Rather should the audience be led to share with the artists on the stage that feeling of ease and naturalness which is an essential concomitant of a truly artistic occasion, in which the spirit of intercommunication never flags.

If much depends upon the accompanist in placing the singer at ease in songs to which composers have not furnished introductions, how much greater becomes the musical responsibility in those significant approaches to many songs which have been supplied by their creators! In many instances the great masters of *Lieder* have designed preludes to their compositions whose structural significance is akin to the imposing vistas through which we glimpse the wonders of a great architectural creation as we approach it. Such moments should be, if not completely revealing, at least clearly prophetic of the wonders to come. The essential spirit of the eventful fulfillment must be sensed at such times, and keen anticipation awakened in both artists and auditors.

Adhering to the purpose of all my quoted musical illustrations, it will be quite sufficient to indicate a few only at this point. The inquiring or informed reader will be able to follow through in the direction indicated with similar instances, as the need arises or curiosity prompts, if he will take the trouble to note a few introductions in which great musical responsibility devolves upon the accompanist. The extent of the accompanist's responsibility will not be comprehended if the approach to song literature is superficial or smacks of routine.

Let me mention in this connection the introduction to Schubert's impressive song, *Der Wanderer*. The composer has given the markings at the beginning: $p < fz$. If these are taken literally, the spaciousness of the beginning, foreshadowing the wonders of the distant lands so dear to the heart of the wanderer, will not be realized. And, for practical purposes, the singer will be totally unprepared, emotionally, for the magnificent opening phrase with its imposing arch. In this case, I begin *piano*, as marked, making a very gradual *crescendo,* but with such unfolding tonal grandeur that the cumulative height attains a spacious *fortissimo,* only lessening the tonal volume gradually as the singer is about to begin. Without such treatment, the great proportions and emotional significance of one of the matchless creations of Schubert's genius would not be realized.

A similar example comes to light in *Die Allmacht,* also by Schubert. Here the piano introduction must convey in a brief space of time the feeling of grandeur, immensity, and awe expressed in the opening words, "Great is Jehovah, the Lord." The accompanist must not merely supply, in this case, the spiritual introduction to an experience, but the very grandeur of the awesome words and Schubert's magnificent phrases. Consequently, the tonal volume of the pianist's introduction must attain an immensity which in some degree conveys the all-pervading spaciousness of the cosmic emotions implicit in words and music. It is only when the singer is about to begin that the vocal entrance is to be foreshadowed by a gradual lessening of tonal intensity.

In marked contrast to these two examples, is a song such as Schubert's simple but deeply poetic *Nacht und Träume*. The blissful unreality of poetic night and equally poetic dreams must be evoked by the accompanist in the introductory phrases so that the eventual realization of the magic of words and music are summed up, as it were, in the piano prelude.

In the three instances quoted in the foregoing, the accompanist's art is subjected to the severest tests. In such fleeting moments he must attain the greatest heights or express the most poetic, subjective emotions, as the case may be. The very brevity of these passing moments makes the task of the accompanist all the greater. So much must be said in so short a space of time, and all too soon he must yield his brief moment of complete emotional expression to artistic collaboration with the soloist.

As the accompanist must be prepared at all times

to pave the way, as it were, for the safe and easy entrance of the singer, he should also gain knowledge and experience in order to make appropriate suggestions concerning the choice of opening numbers for song recitals. The all-important first group, because of faulty judgment on the part of both singer and accompanist, all too frequently presents difficulties for the soloist which overtax both breath control and emotional capacity. The first impression derived by an audience from an unfortunate beginning is something very difficult to overcome as a recital progresses, no matter what heights eventually may be reached. This is a problem which should not be solved by reduction to rigid formula, since, as in many other problems we have considered and will discuss, "circumstances alter cases."

However, the most advantageous selection of an opening group for a singer is invariably one which does not contain songs in which the phrases are long. At the same time the element of spaciousness should be present. Audiences respond most readily to a religious song in the beginning. Such an opening serves as a spiritual prelude, putting performers in the vein and the audience in a receptive frame of mind. The bright, happy type of song also serves well as the introduction to a recital. Great emotional depths and heights should be equally avoided. One regular attendant at song recitals over a period of years was heard to remark that he had never heard Mozart's *Alleluia* adequately sung, since it was always included in the first group and the demands of its long unbroken phrases, so early in the program, placed the singer at a decided disadvantage.

The playing of recitatives in recital programs poses some very important considerations—especially since they are frequently neglected, or, at times, even omitted by performers. It is most inappropriate to perform an aria, either from opera or oratorio, without including the dramatic situation, expressed in recitative, leading up to it. This essential approach to the contrasted lyricism of the aria must not only be included at all times, but it must receive very special and appropriate treatment according to its character. This is particularly to be observed in the performance of dramatic excerpts from the works of Bach, Händel, and Mozart. The recitative, as explanation of a dramatic situation, or, one might say, its justification, must be invested with due importance. Too fast a tempo may rob the recitative of its essential dramatic character, thus failing to prepare the audience psychologically for the ensuing aria. And, at the end of the recitative, the accompanist must close, not concurrently with the singer, but after the soloist has concluded the final vocal phrase. This is an essential consideration sometimes unobserved by arrangers, singers, or accompanists—even, at times, by all three!

In the third chapter entitled *Suiting the Action to the Word*, I cited certain instances when the piano postlude should sustain the climax of the singer's final phrases. It will be noted that these postludes were relatively short. There are many songs in the literature where the postludes are extended, sometimes in the nature of a lengthy coda, in which such sustaining of mood would be very undesirable. I have found that some singers have an antipathy for these extended endings, and, having finished singing, object to the prolongation of the song beyond the point at which they stopped.

An amusing instance of this once occurred in my experience in connection with Richard Strauss' *Heimliche Aufforderung*. Although the singer's final phrase is marked to end *pianissimo,* the Wagnerian tenor Lauritz Melchior chose to ignore the poetic implication of the text in which the words envisage a blissful night reinforced by a prolonged postlude, which ends similarly in a dream-like manner. He insisted on ending the song with a tremendous tonal outburst. Strauss, hearing this later, said to me: "If the singer sings loud, instead of as a poet, you must also end loud. But then you must end with the singer. *Do not play the postlude.*" Thus, in such a contingency, Strauss realized the utter futility of playing the postlude as written, either *pianissimo* or *fortissimo*.

In principle, however, I am averse to making any cuts whatsoever in postludes to songs, no matter how greatly they are extended. The composer has first right to this esthetic treatment, and this seems to me much more valid than that which may be imposed by the performer. Consequently, in such works as Tschaikowsky's *Pilgrim's Song* and Hugo Wolf's *Er ist's*, the long closing sections, played by the piano alone, should be executed as written, although the singer, having finished in both instances with a great climax, must remain vocally inactive while the accompanist has the difficult task of executing an extended recession from the great emotional climax of the vocal soloist. Needless to say, the esthetic purpose of the composer will not be convincingly realized unless the "vocally inactive" singer remains *en rapport* with the music until the accompanist has finished. This is frequently one of the most difficult tasks for a singer, unless the emotional and musical development are equal to the vocal! Julia Culp was one of the few artists equal to such an occasion. At the time Hugo Wolf's *Er ist's* was new to the public, she was aware of what might happen when she had sung the final dramatic outburst, with the piano postlude yet to come. So, when she had finished the concluding phrase, Culp indicated very quietly by manner and gesture that the audience was not to applaud. Audiences were soon so trained that whenever she sang *Er ist's*, many in the hall quickly silenced the uninitiated, and the applause did not ensue until I had concluded the extended *diminuendo* of the postlude.

Early in my career I had occasion, through a very disagreeable experience, to learn the importance of these observations. I was accompanying the Wagnerian tenor Ernest van Dyck in a recital at Wigmore Hall, London. Schumann's *Ich grolle nicht* was to bring a group to a close. At the final phrase van Dyck sang with great power, and before he had finished the last word, *nicht,* I heard a few handclaps. Turning towards van Dyck, I was horrified to see that, simultaneously with his closing phrase, he was executing an elaborate bow, the end of which was carefully timed to coincide with the final word. Whereupon he left the stage. This was an unforeseen contingency, as no mention had been made in rehearsal of omitting the dramatic climax of Schumann's piano postlude. Without losing my poise, I decided in a flash that the only way to save *Ich grolle nicht* from such esthetic desecration was to close the song as Schumann had indicated in the music. Not only did I do this, but, under the great emotional stress of the moment, I played with such power and dramatic intensity that the fugitive hand claps were immediately silenced, until I had finished. Thereupon pandemonium broke loose in the hall, with wild acclaim for the song and the accompanist, and also an implied rebuke to the singer which did not go unnoticed by the critics of the daily press.

But the scene which ensued back stage, where the enraged van Dyck expressed all of his fury, is best left undescribed. And although this could scarcely be termed a happy ending, my solution was, at least, in consonance with Schumann's musical intentions. So I was not too unhappy about it!

CHAPTER VI

THE WELL-TEMPERED ACCOMPANIST

I HAVE already had occasion to mention that "feeling of ease and naturalness" which must be present on the stage, if the receptivity of the audience, engendered by a spirit of intercommunication of artists and public, is completely to be realized. Such an ideal state of affairs may only be achieved by attention to the most minute details on the part of the performers, and, more particularly, on the part of accompanist as performer. Full *rapport* may not be brought about by the best of intentions without careful preparation. It took me many years to foresee and be forewarned of any possible contingency in concert. But even with awareness that "anything can happen" in public performance, and with all precautions taken, the accompanist must be conditioned to meet any and all occurrences, whether foreseen or unforeseen, with good grace.

Early in my career, around the turn of the century, I was engaged to play for a singer who was giving her first Berlin recital. Unfortunately, owing to my limited public experience, I had failed to become acquainted with the piano on which I had to play. Opening with the preliminary chords of the recitative to Haydn's *In Verdure Clad*, I found that many of the keys stuck. Coming to a stop, I quietly told the singer she would have to go backstage until I had found a solution to the problem. The stage attendant suggested that I use another piano which was in the hall. So we started the recitative again. This time, although the keys did not stick, the piano was so badly out of tune that I realized we could not possibly continue. And, again, I had to request the singer to leave the stage.

There was no tuner present, no mechanic; the situation seemed desperate. I asked the attendant if he had a screwdriver. Fortunately he found one. And, having little expectation that my efforts would prove successful, I got down on the floor in my formal evening dress, in full view of the audience, and detached the board in front of the keys. My guess had been right. The board was swollen from dampness so that it jutted against the keys of the piano, holding them down when struck. And, although I was somewhat dishevelled, if not unnerved, the recital continued to a successful conclusion!

This test of my resourcefulness was not to be repeated! However, I had learned the necessity of informing myself beforehand of the condition of the instrument upon which I had to play. This is, sometimes, a disconcerting experience, since care is not generally taken to see that the instrument is in perfect condition for accompanists, who do not re-

Elena Gerhardt

ceive the same consideration accorded soloists. However, no matter what the state of the piano placed at the disposal of the accompanist, and no matter to what extent he is inwardly perturbed, he must under no circumstances permit his emotions to be known to soloist or audience. Every contingency must be met by the accompanist with an outward manifestation of good manners. Any obtrusion of an upset state of mind into the supersensitive atmosphere of an artistic occasion may upset that delicately balanced equilibrium which must be maintained at all times in the relations of artists and the public. And the mere outward show of good manners is not sufficient. It must be actuated by a sensitive consideration of the highly important but equally unobtrusive part he must play, and by that spirit of constant, sympathetic collaboration which comes only from an inner grace.

The "minute attention to details" as a preliminary to a recital involves a careful, orderly arrangement of music. For another unexpected contingency, as I learned somewhat painfully, may arise from the absence of a page of printed notes. All scores should be checked before a concert to avoid such an occurrence. Just such an embarrassing situation arose when I was playing a recital for Elena Gerhardt some years ago. It happened when the famous soprano was singing Brahms' *Blinde Kuh*. The title of the song suddenly took on an implication not foreseen by either poet or composer, when I found myself forced to play, as well as I could, the music of the missing page from memory, although I had not consciously memorized it. Fortunately, my familiarity with the music was such that I was able to cope with the situation without halting the singer. And, most important of all, the audience was unaware of the contretemps!

I have found that the singer in no case should be permitted to assume responsibility for the music, and this goes also for encores. I make it a habit to place the music for each group of songs in a separate pile, in the sequence in which they are to be sung. All pages must be arranged for convenient turning, "dog-earing" the corner of the lower right hand page. I have found it inadvisable to have a third person on the stage during the performance, to turn pages. For this extra presence injects a personality into the stage picture completely unrelated to the nature of the occasion. Furthermore, the properly prepared accompanist has no need of page-turner as assistant.

"Properly prepared" by no means stops at the arrangement of music in groups, etc. It also requires that the accompanist be so familiar with the most advantageous moments for turning the pages that he knows from memory the phrases immediately before and after turning. Frequently I do not turn the music, for fear of losing the smooth continuity of passages or phrases, until the music has progressed well into the following page. And, although I am averse to playing without music in accompanying, for reasons yet to be considered, I am not dependent solely upon the printed page. In fact, if the music were removed, the "play would go on."

Obviously the arrangement of the music for each group in separate piles is possible only when the songs are in sheet music form. If the songs are in volumes, I do not insert sheets of paper to indicate their various places, as many accompanists do, for fear they may fall out. Instead, I note on the front cover of each volume the page and name of the songs to be performed. A further precaution is advisable, in case the singer decides, at the insistence of the audience, to repeat a song. While the singer is acknowledging the applause I always turn to the next song to be sung, at the same time taking care to retain the place of the song just finished, in the event the singer should indicate a repetition.

In arranging the music for encores, it is not sufficient that the sequence be that chosen by the soloist. The singer may decide to alter the choice of encore on the spur of the momet. In fact, since adherence to rigid programming is dispensed with at such times, spontaneity and free choice should be uppermost. Hence, I always arrange the encores in the sequence chosen by the soloist, but in such a manner that the titles show. In this way I can easily extract any encore the singer decides upon.

Perhaps it may seem to some that the foregoing instructions possess much *trivia* which do not require particularization. On the contrary, the smooth running mechanism of public performance demands the utmost attention to these and other seemingly inconsequential items. To quote the familiar definition of Michael Angelo: "Trifles make perfection, and perfection is no trifle."

Since one of the chief functions of the accompanist is to inspire confidence in the singer, his every act and very manner should tend towards producing this result. In fact, this "confidence" is the *sine qua non* of every public recital. Its intangibility is equalled only by its contagiousness. The utmost in artistic achievement may never be attained without the audience coming under the quiet, all-pervading influence of that confidence, born of ease and conviction, which emanates from artists fully aware of their great responsibility to their art and to the public, and equally prepared to meet it. Having had this responsibility instilled in me from my earliest days, by precept and experience, I have never chosen to adopt the custom of playing accompaniments from memory in public. I believe that its adoption militates against the achievement, in the highest degree, of the ability to inspire confidence in the singer.

It is true that the accompanist's familiarity with the music should be so complete that dependence upon music on the printed page is reduced to a minimum. Nevertheless, the music should be available on the stage when needed, and the place for it is on the piano rack. In my career I have found that the need for music, even with the greatest artists, may arise at the most unexpected moment. The singer may be subject to momentary lapse of memory, either of text or music, and a glance at the printed page is sufficient to tide over such an exigency without serious detriment to the sum total of performance. Likewise, the accompanist himself is by no means exempt from similar danger, should he not have the notes before him. And in the accompanist's case, such a defection might seriously affect the poise of the soloist.

In addition to reasons of safety, and the maintenance of the perfect balance and assurance which in large part inspire confidence in performers, it has always seemed to me that playing without notes tends towards an exhibitionism which is contrary to the true character of the ideal accompanist. To play the part of a "show off" does not come properly within the scope of the accompanist's function. As in other procedures which I have suggested, there may be extenuating circumstances that make it peculiarly appropriate to appear on the stage without music. I recall such an instance when Julia Culp included a group of songs by Erich Wolf, long her accompanist, as a tribute to his passing. The unusual, personal nature of the occasion was given a special significance by dispensing with the formality of music for that part of the recital given "in memoriam."

In sonata playing, with violinists or 'cellists, one should always keep in mind the fact that the pianist is not playing an accompaniment, but is the co-equal of the string player. It is frequently observed that violinists, in particular, play sonatas from memory, in the manner of a soloist, while the pianist plays from notes. Such artists as Spalding and Kreisler are never guilty of this error in taste. Either, both pianist and string player should use notes; or, else, both should play from memory. In my estimation, the former is the preferable procedure.

Any mannerisms on the part of an ensemble player which call undue attention to himself easily become a distracting factor to the audience, to the detriment of the music. Not only does this apply to accompanists, but equally to other performers whose musical, if not personal, success depends upon artistic collaboration with others. Even Horowitz, spending the entire introductory period of the *tutti* of a Brahms concerto in adjusting a piano bench which should have been regulated to suit his needs before the arrival of the audience, is guilty of an inartistic and unprofessional approach to public performance. But such distractions are particularly to be avoided by the accompanist, since the spotlight must not, in the nature of the situation, be turned upon him.

Yet, in spite of the role of self-abnegation which the accompanist plays at all times, recognition should be duly given him by the soloist. I say "duly" advisedly, since, no matter what his just desserts, this recognition should not be given with such frequency that it obtrudes itself into the orderly progress of the recital, with a distracting influence upon the audience. Such public recognition by the soloist of an efficient collaborative artist should be carefully timed to occur at the end of the group preceding the intermission, at the close of the recital, or upon insistent public demand at the conclusion of some particularly taxing number in which the accompanist has distinguished himself. In no case should the accompanist presume to obtrude himself into the stage picture in the recognition of applause, unless invited to do so by the soloist. Even then, his response to such audience recognition should be properly tempered to conform to the part he is called upon to play: never too effusive nor too prolonged.

The refusal of the soloist to grant adequate public recognition to the able accompanist is not only unjust but militates against the complete efficiency of collaborative effort and even, at times, becomes annoying to the public. I recall one occasion when I was impelled to rise from where I was a guest in a box at a Town Hall recital of an eminent singer, and publicly protest her failure to invite her excellent accompanist to partake of acclaim which was not only his due, but was, at least in part, obviously intended for him. The accompanist had played the difficult, exquisitely beautiful accompaniment of Koechlin's *l'Hiver* with such appropriate delicacy and shading, with its exacting *glissandi,* that the audience was unusually warm in its acclaim. The singer acknowledged the applause, without sharing it with the pianist, and finally responded to the continued plaudits of the audience by repeating the song. This time, again, the acclaim was unmistakably primarily for the accompanist. And still the *prima donna* continued to bow, entirely oblivious, at least to all outward appearances, that she was aware of the enthusiastic approval of the audience for the remarkable playing of the accompanist.

I asked for and received permission from my hostess to stand and loudly request that the singer include the pianist in the reception of the applause. In the nick of time I was saved from what I was about to do by the soloist finally bringing her accompanist out with her, at the conclusion of the recital and in response only to insistent, prolonged applause of the audience. But her particularly ungenerous attitude, even then, in no way atoned for her complete failure to acknowledge his distinguished services during the course of the recital. Such exclusion of the accompanist from participation in that acclaim which fans the flame of public performance may well prove disheartening to the most able assisting artist, no matter how loyal and self-effacing.

Nevertheless, in these, as well as other predicaments in which the accompanist may find himself, he must be so disciplined that he can cope, at least with apparent ease, with all eventualities, foreseen or unforeseen. And, at all times, his stage behavior must be above reproach. No matter how poor the singer, no matter how uncomfortable he may feel because the vocalist sings off pitch or with excessive *tremolo*, never by look, manner, or gesture must he give any outward manifestation of being aware of these defections. On the contrary, he must train himself always to meet such demands upon his resourcefulness with inspiring ease and confidence. This is the real test of the accompanist's ability and value. And it holds true even if the singer has coached with the accompanist. The relation of teacher and pupil must be abandoned the moment singer and pianist have appeared together before the audience.

It cannot be too often stated that although many unforeseen contingencies may and, unfortunately, do arise in public performance, the accompanist must learn from rehearsals with soloists to be prepared for any eventuality. In rehearsal, particular attention should be paid to uncertainties on the singer's part, arising from any cause: whether from vocal weakness, faulty breathing, loss of memory, or musical deficiency. The accompanist must keep in mind any such defections in rehearsals since these may become, in public performance, even more marked, and certainly more catastrophic. Under these circumstances, the accompanist must virtually be a prestidigitator who is, for instance, capable of making a sudden and unplanned retard; of tarrying longer than required on a fermata; of furnishing a musical cue; even of improvising and stalling for time, until the singer has remembered or recovered poise. All of this must be done so unobtrusively and with no outward sign of perturbation, that the public may not be aware of any unintentional occurrence.

Of course, there are cases when nothing can be

done to save face for the soloist. Although I make a practice of a complete rehearsal of all songs before public performance, and consider this procedure indispensable, it once happened that Julia Culp arrived in New York so late (she had been singing in London) that she decided to leave one song unrehearsed, just prior to her New York recital. The song was *In dem Schatten meiner Locken*, Hugo Wolf's setting of a poem by Paul Heyse. It happens that Brahms also used this same poem as the text of his *Spanisches Lied*. In the midst of the song Madame Culp began singing intervals, even words, not in Wolf's score, with such dissonant effect that all I could think of was that she had suddenly gone crazy. I tried to be as resourceful as possible, but had no clue to guide me. However, this was a hopeless case. I kept on playing, but the effect was terrible! It seems that Brahms, in his setting of the text, repeated the words *Ach nein!* three times, whereas Wolf used the exclamation once only. Madame Culp had just sung Brahms' *Spanisches Lied* in London, and since it was fresh in her mind, became confused in the Wolf song and sang *Ach nein!* three times instead of once. The whole recital was marred by an accident which completely unnerved even so experienced and consummate an artist as Julia Culp.

Although I have, fortunately, always possessed an intuition as to approaching mistakes on the part of soloists, I have learned not to depend upon being forewarned by instinct but to make every preparation to be alert in warding off such contingencies. Deviations from scheduled procedure on the part of the singer should be covered as far as possible by impromptu assistance from the pianist. If the singer is in bad voice, I adjust my tone accordingly, strengthening weak spots by playing louder than is customary. Similarly, I endeavor to make any mistake of the singer inaudible to the audience. Although it is practically impossible to reduce to formula this coping with the unpredictable, the alertness and resourcefulness of the accompanist must be equal to any and all exigencies. This is the reason I am in favor of the "permanent accompanist." Only through long and protracted mutual understanding may the ideal accompanist be developed.

Although the experienced accompanist may be qualified to coach singers in general repertoire, principles of musicianship and everything that pertains to the art of the interpretive musician, I believe it a great mistake and an injustice to singers for the accompanist to become a teacher in the training of voices. I say this knowing full well that I am attacking a very common practice, and one which many of my own pupils have followed. In the occasional advertisements I place with relation to my teaching I insert the clause: *Not a Voice Teacher*. And if vocal defects of production are evident in the singing of pupils, I say: "Go to your singing teacher."

I have seen so much damage result to young voices (and this, unfortunately, is not mitigated by time or maturity) from studying vocal technique with accompanists who are not singers, no matter how extensive their musical knowledge and experience, that I must repeat the ancient injunction to all accompanists: "Shoemaker, stick to your last!" The intricacies of vocal technique are so important, and not so easily imparted or grasped, that I even believe that young singers should study with teachers (and singers) of their own sex and type of voice, if possible—men with men, and women with women.

Occasionally the accompanist may be afforded an opportunity to play solos. Although this may offer him a long awaited opportunity to be a public performer in his own right, as it were, he must not seize the opportunity to "steal the show." His sense of relationship to the whole must not change because of this interlude. Solos chosen for such occasions should neither be too elaborate nor too long. A maximum of ten minutes duration is sufficient. Encores should not be played without deferring to the soloist, and the singer's generosity in granting permission to play an encore should never be taken advantage of to the extent of prolonging the response of the audience by yielding to its demand, if such is the result, of playing more than one encore. It should always be kept in mind that the nature of the recital has to do, first and last, with the performance of the soloist, and that any deviations from this are of only passing moment and may not be prolonged or given undue importance.

In considering the finely adjusted balance which must be constantly maintained between soloist and accompanist, it is not extraordinary that the career of accompanist is seldom undertaken with great distinction by women. The relation of a woman as accompanist to a male singer would demand a reversal of the usual consideration shown the gentler sex. The public spectacle of the woman deferring to the man is so contrary to the usual natural procedure that it becomes too ludicrous for public consumption. The self-abnegation so essential to the role of the accompanist, whether for male or female soloist, demands subdued dress, both in design and color, and the female accompanist is called upon to relinquish something most dear to her heart, and to relegate her charm, both natural and cultivated, to the background. Under the circumstances, it is too much to expect; and could scarcely be demanded. However, as in all other generalities, there are exceptions.

The rigorous discipline necessary to the development of the proficient accompanist, and the strict observance of the procedures I have outlined, by no means constitute the sum total of his existence. As in other walks of life and branches of the musical profession, the law of compensation is in effect, and the rewards are many, in addition to the pecuniary.

Many years ago I waited at a railroad station in Denver, Colorado, to greet my dear friend, the pianist Leopold Godowsky, who was scheduled to arrive by train at 1:30 A.M. At two o'clock he arrived, weary and lonely. In the course of our conversation, Godowsky said that he envied the accompanist, because he always toured with an agreeable companion and did not have to be constantly by himself both in travel and practice. By contrast with his own life, Godowsky frankly considered that the career of the accompanist was less lonely and arduous. Similar views have been expressed to me by Ignaz Friedmann and other solo pianists, whose social contacts on interminable tours were largely confined to an occasional piano tuner who might travel with them, or to comparative strangers and chance acquaintances they might meet in the various cities.

In looking back over the fifty years of my activity as a professional accompanist, I am deeply aware of the richness which has accrued from my association with many great artists; of the constantly varied interests that have enlivened all my tours. Through these my life has had an adventurous and warmly social quality that has kept me young and zestful in spirit. While the financial reward and the personal glamour may not be as great as for the few soloists who reach the top, those rewards are not the most important that may be experienced. The life of a successful accompanist has its own compensations, and these are not only to be realized in retrospect.

I have endeavored to show in this chapter that the accompanist must keep the well-ordered mechanism of the usual and expected procedure running smoothly at all times, yet at the same time be prepared to meet any eventuality with resourcefulness and the appearance of ease. It helps greatly to adopt the attitude of always "Expecting the unexpected," and not be perturbed when it arises. One may well remember that *"anything* may happen in public concert."

There are times when the unexpected happening may lead to a thrilling musical experience. One such occurrence took place at Albert Hall in London in the year 1903. The event was a concert by the American Negro soprano, Alice Gomez.

As was the frequent custom in those days, the concert was made up of an admixture of groups of songs and orchestral compositions. Gomez began with two groups of songs with piano accompaniment, which were followed by orchestral numbers. After that, more songs were scheduled. During the playing of the orchestra, Gomez said: "I shall sing 'Annie Laurie' for an encore after my next group." At that time I was familiar only with the song repertoire of the European continent, comprising German *Lieder* and some French and Italian songs and arias.

I replied, innocently: " 'Annie Laurie'? I don't know that song. I never even heard of it. Have you the music?"

Gomez was astonished at my ignorance of a favorite song of London audiences, sung by all the great *divas* of the day, usually as an encore. So she said: "It is a very simple song to play. I'll show you how it goes. I *must* sing it! You listen carefully and I am sure you will be able to play it with me."

She closed the door so that the playing of the orchestra would not interrupt our rehearsal. Unfortunately the rehearsal was confined to her humming the tune of "Annie Laurie," and my listening, as there was not a piano in the artists' room. But I listened carefully, and soon realized that my problem was not going to be too difficult. I could hear the simple harmonies, as she sang, resolve themselves into a sequence of basic chords: the tonic, or C-major triad; the sub-dominant, from F; the dominant, from G. I was prepared for the inevitable!

After Gomez' next group came the expected encore. Valiantly I went on the vast stage of the great Albert Hall, before an audience of thousands, to play an accompaniment for a song I had not even heard performed! We began, I playing the solid C-major chord. I followed at the various intervals with the other appropriate chords, as I had heard them in the fleeting moment of backstage rehearsal. I played them all solidly, and I was overjoyed to hear that they fitted with the music and that Gomez was singing with assurance.

She then sang the second verse. I now began to feel confidence, and for the second verse, instead of playing the chords solidly, I improvised a simple figuration: playing a bass octave followed by a distribution of the harmonic tones into an eighth note pattern. This sounded even better than the first time! My ease and assurance were now complete.

We began the third verse. I started to repeat the simple device I had improvised for the second verse. As we proceeded, I saw the old German orchestral conductor, now standing in the wings, trying to attract my attention. He was so greatly in earnest, that I watched him intently to see what he wanted, at the same time playing on without interruption. As Gomez' voice soared, the conductor cupped his hands and, in a loud stage whisper, fairly shouted: "A minor." I played the A-minor harmony called for. It sounded all right! The old man was getting more excited. Now came the command: "D minor." No sooner said than done. And it sounded still better!

I did not know where I was going next, harmonically speaking, but so far so good! The old conductor was now in a very fever of excitement as he called: "E major." With a glorious burst came the brilliant, unexpected harmony. Gomez sang divinely. The old man was applauding silently but furiously. The verse was finished. I was flushed with excitement and success!

The fourth and final verse now began. I had served my novitiate in regard to "Annie Laurie." I now realized the possibilities, and for the finale I improvised a brilliant accompaniment of arpeggios. At the conclusion came cheers and tumultuous applause. The old conductor embraced me. Gomez could only say: "Wonderful! Wonderful!"

CHAPTER VII

THE ACCOMPANIST AS COACH

THE strictures I have made on accompanists presuming to teach vocal technique in spite of the fact that they are themselves without practical singing training or experience by no means apply to the giving of professional advice to vocal soloists in matters of style, musicianship, including all the term implies, and so-called interpretation. On the contrary, the accompanist who, in addition to adequate academic training, has had the privilege of playing extensively for many of the greatest artists of all time, and has consequently learned the secrets of their artistic achievements, is under an obligation to share the treasures accruing from his varied experiences with others.

Hence, I have repeated some of my most enjoyable and rewarding musical experiences in passing on to singers and accompanists those principles of the art of song which I have found to be essential to their artistic development, in courses given in colleges and schools of music, as well as in private instruction.

Most of the essentials of the art may be explained and illustrated without too great difficulty. The principle which I consider the most important one of all, I have come to reserve until the final lesson of the course. It not only furnishes the peak of the artistic structure gradually developed over a period, but it is the most difficult to impart. In fact, its presentation poses such problems that I have customarily introduced this all-important artistic principle with a prelude designed to accentuate its significance. It is to me the "pearl of great price" which reveals one of the rarest beauties of the vocalists' art. I refer to the principle of the *slur*.

Through its extravagant application and long misuse, especially in Italian opera, a stigma has come to attach itself to the very word "slur." We frequently hear someone remark, or even ourselves say, of a singer: "She (or he) slurred"—as if this were a term of opprobrium. The truth of the matter is that there are good and bad slurs; slurs which add to the inherent emotion of texts and music if properly executed—and, conversely, slurs which transform sentiment into mawkish, exaggerated sentimentality and create disgust and revulsion of feeling in the sensitive, discriminating listener. In fact, the importance of the properly executed and timed slur is so great that the singing of many of the greatest singers and most famous artists has been seriously marred by lack of its comprehension and application.

My attention was first called to the effective and esthetically right use of the slur and its faulty application in Hugo Wolf's *Verborgenheit*. When I played this song for von Zur-Mühlen, at the words *seine Wonne, seine Pein*, the singer slurred with such convincing emotion that no one could possibly question its appropriateness. Later, when I played this same song for Ludwig Wüllner, he also slurred at the same point. But the result in Wüllner's case was neither convincing nor effective. In fact, it sounded so bad to me that I endeavored to discover the great difference between the two manners of executing the slur and the resulting difference in interpretive effect. The existing disparity may best be exemplified by singing. But it may also be explained by the following examples, together with the analysis which follows:

Example 1

sei - ne Won - - - ne, sei - ne Pein!

Example 2

sei - ne Wonn - - e, sein - e Pein!

It will be noted that the syllabication of Example I is in accordance with the customary division of the words *Won-ne* and *sei-ne*. However, since these two words should be slurred, the division into syllables should be as in Example II, so that the *slur is executed on the consonant, not on the vowel*. In this case the syllabication becomes *Wonn-e* and *sein-e,* respectively. A vocal test will demonstrate the incontestable superiority of Example II, in which the enunciation of the text will not have been marred. And the musical gain is evident.

The method of slurring on consonants may only be practiced when consonants can be hummed, as with *l, m, n, ng*, and *r*. It may never be used effectively with such consonants as *b, t,* or *g*. In other words, slur on *nasal* consonants only.

In Brahms' *Sapphic Ode,* where one syllable of a word is twice carried over several tones, the first time with an *s*, the second time with a nasal consonant, the execution is as follows:

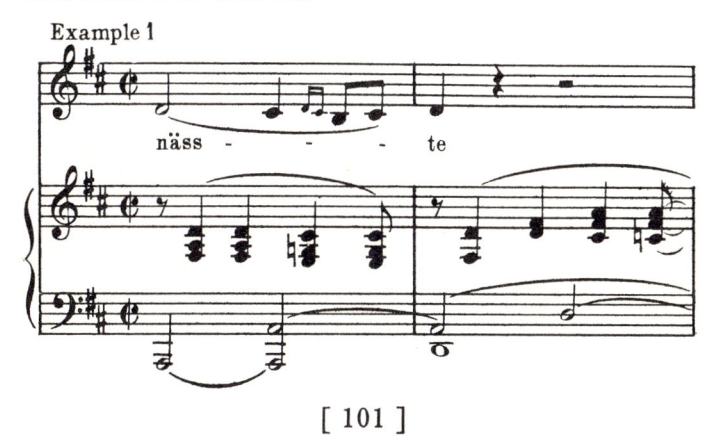

Example 1

näss - - te

Example 2

Thrä - - - n - en.

In Example I there is no slur on the word *nässte*, each syllable of which is to be enunciated with great distinctness, as shown. In Example II, the slur occurs on the vowel until the syllable changes, *Trä-nen* becoming *Trän-en*. The *n* was only added as the syllable changed, as indicated.

Similar instances occur frequently in all languages, not only in German, as will readily be seen in the examples to follow.

When a word finishes with a vowel and is followed with another beginning with a vowel, it is permissible to slur on the open vowel as in *the eyes,* or its German equivalent, *die Augen*. Similarly where a syllable ends with a vowel and is followed by another in the succeeding one, as in *tru-est love*, the two syllables should not be separated with distinctness of enunciation but connected by a slur as shown.

A common error in slurring frequently occurs in the singing of *Elsa's Traum* from *Lohengrin* on the word *heissen* at the phrase: *Will er Gemahl mich heissen.* Here the word *heissen* (*hei-ssen*) should be syllabicated distinctly, without a slur. The correct singing of this phrase is executed by Helen Traubel. In fact, Traubel to a greater degree than any other famous artist of the day has mastered the difficult and vitally important art of the slur in singing. Julia Culp was another singer who invariably treated the slur correctly, with supreme artistic result.

Several years ago when Rose Bampton studied the leading soprano role in *Trovatore* for the Metropolitan, she carefully prepared the moments to be slurred so that their execution was in conformance with the artistic principles which I have used in coaching many of the greatest artists. At rehearsal, Papi, the eminent Italian operatic conductor, recognized the advisability of Bampton's slurring in the right manner, although this was contrary to the abominable custom of singers in the role. However, Papi said that there were a couple of places where she must slur in the usual Italian manner, as the public was so accustomed to the wrong, inartistic way that they could not accept any other style of singing. Bampton's artistic success, however, was so great, that, after the first performance, Papi declared that she should execute all of the slurs in the same, esthetically correct style.

In instances where a word ending in a consonant is followed by another beginning with a consonant, two rules should be observed. The first applies in such a phrase as *hast du mich lieb*. The *t* in hast and the *d* in *du* should be sounded once only, as follows: *hast-du*. This rule is in effect only when the letters of the second word following the initial consonant do not constitute, in themselves, a word. In this case the *u* following *d* (*d-u*) is not a word, but merely a vowel. Similar cases occur with such combination as *bist du*

Mack Harrell and Coenraad V. Bos

and *musst-du*. The other rule applies in the use of the following and similar words: *hast dein* and *und Traum*. In the former instance it will be noted that *d* in *dein* is followed by *ein*, a German word. In the latter, *t* in *Traum* is followed by another German word, *Raum*. In these and similar cases the greatest care must be taken so that the final *d*'s and the initial *t*'s are enunciated separately and distinctly.

It will be seen from the foregoing that there is a time to slur and a time to refrain from slurring; as well as slurs which sound right and musical and those which mar the singing of many artists before the public. In my long experience in coaching, I have had occasion to instruct some young, cold, "white" voices. The results attained in relatively short periods by means of musically correct slurring have astonished everyone who witnessed them. Since the subtle technical differences between correct and incorrect slurring are seldom grasped by the uninitiated, the reaction to the improvement has usually been expressed by the remark: "The singing has become so much more sympathetic." Even the young, cold voice may be imbued with a semblance of warmth through the application of principles whose value is akin to "That pearl of great price." And they have been the most highly treasured artistic possession of some of the greatest singers of today and other days who have learned its value through my instruction, including such artists as Johannes Messchaert, Julia Culp, Anton van Rooy, Maria Mueller, Frieda Hempel, Myra

Frieda Hempel

Mortimer, Rose Bampton, Mack Harrell, and, last but not least, Helen Traubel.

As the artistry of these and other singers has been enriched by means of the properly executed and timed slur, the mastery of which constitutes one of the greatest problems in diction and interpretation, so it has influenced the teaching of many who have attended my classes throughout the years. This was forcefully impressed upon me by an experience in one of my recent summer classes. A young student sang for me so musically, that I remarked, in astonishment: "You have mastered the principle of the slur perfectly. Where did you study?" He replied: "With Alice Moncrieff at the University of Kansas." Then I recalled that some thirty years before, Alice Moncrieff had attended one of my summer college classes!

In my work in coaching many and diverse singers, I have found that it is inadvisable to be rigid in one's conception of *tempo*. It has aptly been said: "It's a wise man who knows his own tempo." Consequently, I make it a rule to ask the singer to indicate the chosen tempo before beginning an introduction, which, in effect, indicates the rate of speed of a song, such as the opening measures of Schubert's *Die Forelle* and *Der Lindenbaum*, and Brahms' *Botschaft*. Any revision of the tempo set by the accompanist at the singer's entrance, may upset the entire balance of the song and rob it of its artistic result. Tempo, by its very nature, varies with the type of voice and temperament of the singer, as well as the intellectual conception, and should not be superimposed by the accompanist. Such diverse rates of speed may properly come within the scope of an indicated tempo, such as *Andante, Allegro, Lebhaft,* etc. Furthermore, accompanists in general are inclined to play too slowly when the designated tempo is slow; and too rapidly when the tempo is fast.

In addition to the principles considered in this chapter there are many other matters of musicianship, diction, and interpretation to be inculcated by the coach. However, the accompanist acting in the capacity of coach to singers, either experienced or inexperienced, must know well the nature of his functions, where they begin and end, as well as their way on the ascent of Parnassus.

Master Class by Coenraad V. Bos

CHAPTER VIII

PROBLEMS OF STYLE

The manner, or style, of playing accompaniments varies, of necessity, under different conditions and circumstances. Here, again, it must be remembered that "circumstances alter cases," and the capabilities of the skilful accompanist must be fairly Protean in coping with varying musical requirements, both of the instrumental support and soloist.

Although accompanists abound in the profession of music, there are few who may be considered first rate. The ones who may be placed in this category must, in spite of that self-abnegation which is their most obvious virtue, possess a broad musicianship which singers seldom attain. In other words, the accompanist must have more extensive and profound knowledge of various styles and their esthetics than the soloist. In fact, he usually does have. But in most cases, this is not saying very much. The properly equipped accompanist must be ready at all times in rehearsal to make suggestions to singers concerning essential differentiations in style inherent in the works of the various masters of song. These variations in style are as diverse and numerous as the times and places, with their widely differing environmental influences, from which the composers and authors of the texts of songs emanate.

On the other hand, the accompanist may learn more from truly great singers than from his teachers of piano. This has certainly been true in my own case. Insight into the appropriate and effective interpretation of great music is something one may derive more readily from practical experience with great singers than from the precepts of the piano studio.

One of the more obvious variations in style of playing to which the accompanist must readily and easily adapt himself, may be comprehended in the consideration of the diverse character of operatic and song literature.

For the greater part, operatic scores in "arrangement" for piano are apt to be literal adaptations, with insufficient attention to the relatively limited capabilities of the instrument to reproduce orchestral effects, and equally limited understanding of the piano idiom. Few, indeed, are the effective, musically just arrangements of operatic scores for piano! The most notable achievements in this respect are the Klindworth piano arrangements of Wagner's orchestral scores of the music-dramas. While these esthetically right examples come readily to mind, the number of instances in which orchestral adaptations for piano degenerate into claptrap is so great that it would be impracticable, as well as unnecessary, to list them.

For our purposes, it is only advisable to cite two

comparative illustrations, one good and one poor, of accompaniments to an aria: Beethoven's *Freudvoll und leidvoll* from *Egmont*. In the Peters Edition, the thin, unidiomatic piano arrangement of this aria is musically ineffective, whereas in the edition of Breitkopf and Härtel that of Carl Reinecke is richer, and more faithfully conveys Beethoven's musical intentions through the medium of the piano. I recommend a study of these two arrangements to all accompanists who would successfully cope with the problem of playing adaptations of orchestral scores on the piano.

Similarly, the accompanist must view all orchestral scores in transcription for piano with a certain amount of suspicion, and not hesitate to make changes which result in greater effectiveness—so long as no damage is done the inherent musical meaning and structure of the original scores.

One of the commonest faults of "arrangers" of operatic scores for piano occurs in the indiscriminate use of the *tremolo*, eminently suited to the strings of the orchestra where its effectiveness is frequently matched by its unobtrusiveness. On the piano, such effects must be used with the utmost economy, and played with consummate skill. Otherwise, an element not apparent in an orchestral rendition emerges with glaring, cheapened result. It is virtually impossible to reproduce orchestral *timbres* on the piano, and the less the accompanist tries to do this, the better.

Arrangements from operatic scores of coloratura passages frequently call upon the pianist to play in unison with the singer. This is an error in taste characteristic of many arrangers. It is impossible to blend such a paralleling of the singer's musical line, in the piano accompaniment, with that fusion of vocal and instrumental tone which is accomplished when the orchestral version is used. I do not hesitate to rearrange such passages, being careful to give sufficient support to the singer, without a futile attempt to imitate an orchestral instrument. Such a course should be followed, without hesitation, by all professional accompanists.

Faulty arrangements are by no means confined to operatic selections. They are also frequently to be found in folksongs. Both over-elaboration and over-simplification of the accompaniments to folk songs are equally to be avoided, and here, again, the accompanist should not hesitate to make alterations in the piano part. What must be remembered in making changes in the accompaniments of such simple songs is that the piano should furnish ample but stylistically correct support to the soloist, without calling undue attention to the accompaniment. Here a knowledge of styles, based upon what is esthetically right, is absolutely necessary.

The principal concessions I make in playing accompaniments to operatic arias are in the nature of greater freedom, a wider dynamic range, and appropriate accents of dramatic nature which would, generally speaking, amount to exaggeration in accompanying songs or German *Lieder*.

Relatively speaking, the accompaniments of songs and *Lieder* written originally for piano require a much "purer" style of playing; a more exacting attention to detail as indicated by composers; less accent upon musico-dramatic "effects" than the larger, more spectacular canvas of opera demands. In the finer, more intimate atmosphere of song, the sensitivity of the original creator must be recreated without undue emphasis or exaggeration. But here, paradoxically, more and finer tonal and dynamic gradations are required within circumscribed limits than in opera. This applies also to the essential differences in style of the two species.

The "differences in style" emerge clearly from a study of the character of masters of the *Lied*, such as Schubert, Schumann, and Brahms. Schubert and Schumann require a "pure" style, in consonance with their musical natures. In playing Brahms, however, I use a deeper tone, greater intensity. "Purity" of style, with Brahms, is not the dominant factor. Naturally, such distinctions cannot and should not be reduced to formula, or considered as all-embracing generalizations. There are too many exceptions occurring in the *Lieder* of all three masters to make it possible to approach their compositions with any general, preconceived ideas as to the style of their interpretations. While there is a preponderance of certain highly individual characteristics in the inherent style of the *Lieder* of each of these great composers, every one of their songs must receive special study and analysis by the accompanist in terms of itself, if a really complete understanding of its meaning—hence style—is to be realized.

For instance, there are widely divergent styles requiring appropriately different tonal treatment, to be found within the works of each of these masters. This will be readily comprehended by placing in close juxtaposition, for the moment, such *Lieder* as Schubert's *Erl König* and the same master's *Die Forelle*; Schumann's *Du bist wie eine Blume* and his *Stille Thränen*; Brahms' *Der Todt das ist die kühle Nacht* or *Immer leiser wird mein Schlummer* and *Von ewiger Liebe* or *Der Schmied*. Such comparisons, which might well be carried on indefinitely, demonstrate the necessity for differentiation existing *within* the works of these, as well as other masters' songs; in addition to essential stylistic distinctions of a general nature to be adduced from comparing the musical utterances of various composers.

Supplementing the foregoing generalizations regarding "style," I am impelled to speak of several specific instances in which stylistic shortcomings are most frequently to be perceived in the playing of accompaniments. These examples will also serve to indicate the utmost care and perception that must be brought to the study of each and every song by the accompanist who would become a master-craftsman.

A common error is to be found in the playing of Brahms' *Der Schmied*. The right hand figure, repeated throughout the song, comprises, as will be observed, a sixteenth note, an eighth note, and a sixteenth rest, as follows:

[musical notation: "Ich hör' mei-nen Schatz, den"]

This constitutes merely a naturalistic, exact reproduction of the rhythm, action, and reaction, which Brahms must have carefully noted in the swinging of a heavy hammer by a blacksmith. The first, or sixteenth, note is where the hammer strikes; the second, or eighth, note is the repercussion from the blow upon the anvil; the sixteenth rest is the interval in which the hammer is raised for the next blow, to be struck "while the iron is hot." The accompanist must execute this reiterated figure with the same realistic, percussive effect as that achieved, perforce, by the competent smith. Most frequently one hears the initial tone of the figure played fleetingly as a short *appoggiatura*, and with insufficiently percussive accent, so that the imitative effect of the hammer's blow (action) and the ensuing rebound and repercussion (reaction) are not achieved. I realize, of course, that there was greater opportunity, in Brahms' day, to see and hear a blacksmith in action. But this is only one of many instances where the accompanist is called upon to have a fertile imagination. And it is just this which may save the day for the performers, even in the absence of actual experience and training in the correct and accurate presentation of particular sounds.

Another notable instance in which accompanists frequently fail to achieve an effect essential to the realization of the composer's intentions and the inherent meaning of the music occurs in Brahms' *Auf dem Kirchhofe*. In the playing of the repeated figure, made up of eight 32nd notes culminating in a chord, I frequently get the impression that the accompanist has practiced his arpeggios not wisely, but too well. This reiterated pattern, the example of which follows, is not to be arpeggiated glibly or superficially, with too much damper pedal. On the contrary, every tone of the 32nd note figure must emerge with the utmost distinctness, and the ensuing chord must rest upon a seemingly solid, stalwart base, or bass. Care must be taken that the damper pedal is not used to blur the eight note figure so that individual tones fail to sound clearly. Each tone should be played *forte*, as indicated:

A very different stylistic problem confronts the accompanist in Schubert's *Die Stadt*. Here the eerie tonal effect to be achieved will result in the inherent creepiness and morbidity of the music and text only if a monochromatic monotony is preserved throughout. The slow *tremolo* of the bass should be played with utmost lightness and mystery. I advise practicing each hand separately until the required result is attained: mystery in left hand; a ghostly, wraith-like quality in the right. Such an effect is not to be achieved primarily through pedal use, but rather by a subtle, accurately balanced tonal control which few accompanists are able to evoke from the piano.

In spite of the fact that the accompanist should adhere as closely as possible to the music as written by the masters of song, there are times when the notation militates against the easy, natural realization of that which the composer intended to express. Such a case arises in the accompaniment to Schubert's *Auf dem Wasser zu singen*. Here Schubert has, by the reiteration of a two-note figure, conveyed the sound of rippling water. In the beginning of the song, it is a simple matter for the technically proficient accompanist to achieve the desired result, inasmuch as the right hand is concerned only with playing single notes, unimpeded by the addition of harmony which is carried in the bass by the left hand. Yet, when Schubert indicated a diminuendo (and the accompanist is responsible for executing a subtle effect) he added harmonic tones in the right hand. The task of achieving an increasingly tenuous tonal texture, with the addition of repeated harmonic tones, poses a musical problem completely out of relation to the difficulty presented. At this point, I play as indicated in Example I. Example II is Schubert's original notation.

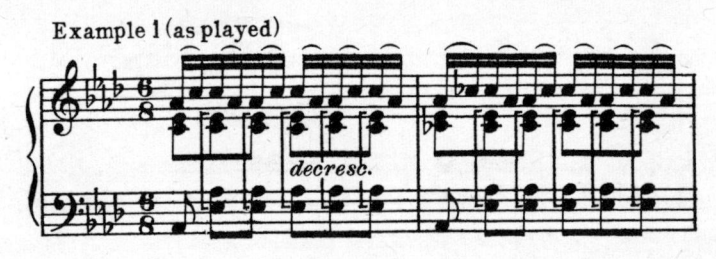

Example 1 (as played)

Example 2 (original)

A playing of these two examples on the piano demonstrates the gain in the easy attainment of the desired result (Example I), when the harmony is sounded in the left hand. In the latter case (Example II), weight was added by Schubert in the right hand when lightness is demanded by the character of the music. There are undoubtedly those whose blind worship of the composer obscures understanding of the difference between unthinking adherence to the *letter* and grasping the essential *spirit* of the music. I have found it to be much more productive to approach such problems with an open mind. The musical gain is apparent when a maximum of effect is attained with a minimum of effort!

The accompanist who is proficient in transposition will be in a much better position to serve the soloist than the one who does not possess talent or training for this important aspect of the art. This is particularly true in song literature. For in the production of opera the problem of transposition does not arise, inasmuch as the keys of various arias must conform to the context and singers are carefully selected for parts which lie well for their voices. There is, because of this, a wider range for the recitalist. All songs may be made available to the competent vocalist, through transposition. Again, we find some who are averse to such changes, since the composer originally wrote each song in one key only. Yet there is plenty of evidence to show that the composers themselves were not always averse to transposition of their songs, provided the rendition gained thereby. Ludwig Wüllner frequently told me of occasions when

Brahms tried many of his songs in various keys, in order to determine the one in which a particular song could be sung most easily and effectively. Since Brahms himself did not hesitate to set such a precedent, there seems to be little or no reason not to follow in the same direction.

Richard Strauss was also a composer who was in favor of changing the keys of songs when the need arose. He, for instance, originally wrote *Cäcilie* in the key of E-major, and later in E-flat. (It is also published in C.) The transposition downwards, here, as in most cases, is preferable. Particularly, in such a song as *Cäcilie,* the extremely high tessitura in the original key makes it almost impossible of satisfactory performance. In lower keys the musical gain is too obvious to require more extended discussion.

It is not sufficient for the accompanist to rely upon the transposition of songs as they are issued by publishing houses. There are too many instances of songs, transposed for publication from the original into keys for "low," "medium," or "high" voices, as the case may be, failing in effectiveness when sung in the altered keys. An instance of this occurs in Brahms' *Immer leiser wird mein Schlummer,* written originally in the key of C-sharp minor. For soprano it has been transposed into the key of F minor. Yet it is, for practical purposes of easy and effective performance, impossible of execution in this key. This is only one of many instances where the transposition of songs as issued by publishers does not serve the accompanist in various situations arising with singers.

Hence, it will clearly be seen from the foregoing that the necessity exists for easy transposition. Note that, generally speaking, transposition *downwards* is preferable. However, in the latter respect, there is only one criterion: *The song must lie right for the singer's voice.*

While I believe that a special talent is required for transposition and that this is an essential of the accompanist's natural equipment, there is no doubt that many have become adept in this respect through rigorous self-discipline and training.

The accompanist must exercise eternal vigilance in being prepared to cope with any exigency that might mar the musical style of the soloist. A few typical illustrations will serve to indicate some of the pitfalls which are bound to occur from time to time. One of these has to do with sudden, dramatic releases of high tones, as in Richard Strauss' *Ruhe, meine Seele*. For appropriate dramatic effect the accompanist should break off the chord simultaneously with the singer's F-sharp. I have found it advisable to release the chord dramatically and abruptly, so that, to the eye, the break of soloist and accompanist synchronizes. But I cover the sudden release of the singer's F-sharp by holding down the damper pedal for an instant, as shown in the following example. Otherwise, the singer's F-sharp, lacking the tonal support of the piano, is apt to sound like a shriek, and the ensuing rest will become an embarrassing silence.

bring-en Herz und Hirn in Not

Another typical moment in which the alert accompanist can save the day for the singer occurs in Strauss' *Sie wissen nicht*. The singer reaches a climax on the tone G, while the pianist plays a diminished 7th chord. After a short interval of rest, the singer is called upon to execute a B-flat, sung piano, without any preparation or cue from the accompanist. Since, on the piano, the singer's B-flat is, enharmonically, the same as the A-sharp of the diminished 7th chord of the climax, I continue holding the A-sharp when the chord is released, so that the singer can hear it and begin the new phrase, starting *piano* on B-flat, with assurance, as indicated:

A similar instance is to be found in *Velvet Shoes*, by the contemporary American composer, Randall Thompson. The piano interlude ends on a C-sharp major triad, with the song continuing immediately in the key of F-major. Since the piano's E-sharp, of the C-sharp major chord, is enharmonically the same as the first tone of the singer's next phrase, F, I retain the single tone E♯, so that what looks like a difficult modulation on paper is actually accomplished without peril for the singer:

In Schubert's *Der Neugierige* we come across one of those difficult psychological problems, derived from the text, which few singers seem to understand. Preceding the words: *O Bächlein meiner Liebe, wie bist du heut' so stumm!*, Schubert has indicated a complete silence, a rest of three eighth notes' duration. Unless the singer exerts the utmost care to observe the full value of these rests, as well as to grasp the significance of the silence, there is no psychological preparation or justification for the words quoted:

This is only one of innumerable instances in which the accompanist's knowledge of song literature must transcend mere familiarity with the notes. It must penetrate into the innermost meanings of the texts, and he must be prepared at all times to share his knowledge with singers whose experience in the art of song is all too frequently derived from emphasis on vocalization.

I have dealt primarily with the nature of problems arising in the accompanying of soloists. However, there are other fertile fields, particularly for the young accompanist, whose fundamental requirements should be understood by those who would prove competent in a branch of the profession requiring great versatility and ability to cope with any situation which may arise.

In accompanying choruses, the singers should be grouped near, preferably around, the piano. While the subtleties of playing for soloists are not so vitally important in choral rehearsal, other considerations arise. One of the principal factors involved in supplying appropriate support for group singing is the "dry" accompaniment, *i.e.*, when the pianist uses the least possible amount of damper pedal. The accompanist should depend primarily upon sustaining the tone with the hand rather than with the pedal. Upper and lower tones should be to the fore and clearly heard, with particular emphasis upon the supporting or bass tones.

The dance, both of soloists and ballet, offers a wide range of opportunity to the accompanist of today. Curiously enough, I have found that most young accompanists hesitate to take positions in dance studios. This hesitation arises frequently from a misconception of the difficulties of playing for dancers. But adjustments to the special requirements of dancing are actually more easily made than in any other branch of accompanying. Here the time element is the principal factor, and the accompanist is required to play, for the greater part, for dance routines whose duration is exactly charted—for instance, for two minutes—more or less—then "cut"! The problem for the accompanist who would preserve his musical ideals becomes one of working out the music for dances in which the time element is dominant, but so that as little damage as possible is done the structure of the music through "cuts." The cuts should be made to conform to the original structure of the music. Much of the "modern" dance music is composed, or rather fashioned, to the requirements of the dance, and in this case no problem is presented. However, in adaptations of existing music for the purposes of a particular dance, the accompanist is confronted with a real test of his musical knowledge and taste. My experiences in accompanying dancers have, perhaps fortunately, been confined to such artists as Anita Berber and Isadore Duncan. These were great artists of such taste and distinction that the association with them leaves only pleasant and treasured memories.

Particularly memorable was my opportunity of playing for Isadora Duncan. My teacher, Röntgen, had been accompanying Duncan in a series of public recitals. When Röntgen became suddenly ill, I was engaged to substitute for him. The great dancer immediately put me at ease, at rehearsal, by remarking: "Play as you wish—I shall follow. I dance to music. You are not to accompany the dance."

How many dancers consider music in this light?

CHAPTER IX

THE HUMAN ANGLE

During the first years of my activity as a professional accompanist I had the good fortune to be associated with some of the greatest artists of what was to me a "golden age." While still very young and relatively unknown, in addition to accompanying such masters of the art of song as von Zur-Mühlen and Johannes Messchaert, I had the privilege of playing publicly for Albani, Rosa Sucher, David Popper, Sarasate, Joachim, and Schumann-Heink. These were all artists of established reputation in the musical world, and the association with them greatly enriched my artistic experience. However, in retrospect, incidents of human interest sometimes take precedence over those of a purely musical nature. These were frequently as revealing of the characters of these musicians, both human and artistic, as their musical accomplishments.

One of the great Wagnerian singers of the Bayreuth Festivals and Berlin Hofoper, the soprano Rosa Sucher retired from the Bayreuth opera in the 1890's, because of declining powers. Since she no longer possessed the physical strength to cope with the arduous demands of the dramatic Wagnerian roles, Frau Sucher planned a series of *Lieder* recitals. She and her husband, Josef Sucher, a famous conductor of the Berlin Hofoper, were, in spite of their eminence in the world of music, in need of funds, and the plan of giving ten *Lieder* recitals seemed to be the best and easiest way to recoup their fortunes. Naturally, as a young and ambitious accompanist at the inception of a career, I was thrilled at being engaged to accompany one of the most beloved and famous singers of the day in such a series, little realizing what the denouément would be.

My initial rehearsal at the home of the Sucher's was a foretaste of what was to come. The first song was Schubert's *Wohin?* The great Wagnerian soprano, no matter what her attainments in the operatic field, was not a great musician, and the requirements of the deceptively simple song were beyond the limits of her experience and knowledge. Sucher's husband, Josef, completely oblivious of my presence, roared at his poor wife: she could not sing in time, even in something as easy as Schubert's *Wohin?* She knew nothing. She could not even count! In short—she was dumb! His berating of his unfortunate wife continued throughout the rehearsal. My presence was completely ignored; at least, it did not deter him from heaping abuse upon her. After all, I was only a young unknown pianist to these famous people. But Frau Sucher's singing certainly did not improve under her husband's tongue-lashing. It could scarcely be called an auspicious beginning.

It was planned to give the first and last recitals in the Beethoven Saal in Berlin, the other eight in various parts of Germany. The first of these events, to which I had looked forward with keen anticipation, took place before a capacity audience. Frau Sucher, no longer at the height of her vocal powers, was rapturously received by her admirers who showed no outward signs of being aware of her shortcomings, all too obvious to everyone present. Even when she sang Wagner's *Träume* as the climax of the recital, and, completely out of breath had, perforce, to breathe after the F on the first syllable of *Träume*, breaking the word and the phrase, the Berlin audience, faithful to the last, refused to manifest any less acclaim. Financially and in warmth of reception the recital was a great success.

The second of Frau Sucher's recitals was given in the small mountain town of Gosslar. The audience here was not composed of faithful followers eager to ignore the shortcomings of a beloved artist no longer in her prime. In spite of the fact that Gosslar was a provincial town far away from the sophisticated public of Berlin, it possessed a musical society whose members took their music very seriously. And this music-loving, rather than hero-worshipping, group of people, listened intelligently, without memories of the artist's former triumphs in mind. The result was complete reversal of the audience's reaction to Sucher's

Berlin recital. After each song and every group, there was a growing chill in the hall. This was even more in evidence, by contrast, when I played a solo group. The audience seemed unnecessarily eager in their applause, evidently in order to show the warmth of their appreciation of my playing, where a moment before they had manifested less than polite tolerance of the pathetic efforts of a singer on the decline.

After the recital, the President of Gosslar's musical society brought a huge autograph album to Frau Sucher to sign, as was the custom when famous artists performed there. Up until this moment, she had given no outward sign of her inner perturbation, although this must have been very great. But now, as she took the book, I realized that she was under great emotional strain. And, when I saw that she was drawing musical lines, making the staff, then adding notes and words, I wondered what she had in mind. It was the custom for celebrated artists to sign such an autograph book with lightness of spirit, and words in similar vein. This was by all signs and portents, however, a moment of tragedy.

And so it proved to be. As Frau Sucher handed the autograph book to the musical organization's President, he, prepared to say the usual conventional words of thanks to the artist, was silenced and dumbfounded as he read: *"Und sinken in die Gruft."* The tragic words "And then sink into the grave," taken by Frau Sucher from the final song of the recital, Wagner's *Träume*, were indeed fateful. The official of the musical society stuttered a few almost incoherent words and, red-faced and embarrassed, closed the book. Frau Sucher, realizing in one tragic moment that her career was ended, cancelled the eight remaining recitals. Thus was the curtain rung down on a distinguished career.

Another of the great singers of other days with whom I was associated towards the end of her public career was the dramatic soprano Emma Albani. Born in Montreal in 1852 where she lived during the first twelve years of her life, Albani may be considered an American singer since she lived for several years in Albany and sang there at the Roman Catholic Cathedral until she went abroad to study with Duprez and Lamperti. She sang with enormous success in the great European opera houses and was also well-known in many countries for her concert singing. She was a particular favorite in England where she ended a notable public career in 1911.

Shortly after the turn of the century I was engaged to accompany Madame Albani in a London recital. One of the principal numbers on the program was Schumann's song cycle *Frauenliebe und Leben*. Up until that time, the singers with whom I had played these masterpieces of the German *Lied* had brought the cycle to a close in a sustained mood of grief. But Albani had a different conception of the finale. At the words *"Der Schleier fällt,"* (The veil drops), she sang with the mournful memory that the husband was dead. At the next phrase *"Da hab' ich dich*," (There I have you), Albani placed her left arm as though she were holding a baby, and smiled lovingly towards the imaginary infant. At the following words "*und mein verlor'nes Glück* (and my lost happiness), the mood again, with the memory of the lost dear one, became one of sadness. And finally, at the closing words "*Du meine Welt*" (You, my world), Albani smiled rapturously at the envisaged child which held the hope of future happiness.

Although Albani brought gestures to assist in conveying the shifting moods of the finale of *Frauenliebe und Leben*, to the audience, after the manner of operatic artists, she executed these with such conviction and simplicity that the artistic result was profoundly moving and eminently appropriate.

Shortly afterwards, when I had occasion to play Schumann's song cycle in Berlin with Schumann-Heink, I told her about Albani's conception of the finale. She was so deeply impressed by it that she immediately changed her style of singing the closing phrases. But where Albani had brought gestures to her assistance, Schumann-Heink by emotional expression and tonal control was able to project the varying moods with even more convincing result. Julia Culp, also, at my suggestion, sang the finale of Schumann's *Frauenliebe und Leben* in similar manner, and, later, Helen Traubel, likewise.

In playing the close of Schumann's cycle, it gradually developed in my mind that the piano postlude, in which the music of the first song of the cycle recurs, would better convey the vision of future happiness, implicit in the final words, if I played this recapitulation in its initial form. I played it this way for Schumann-Heink, and she was so pleased with the result that I have continued to use this version of the postlude ever since. And, in the various criticisms I have received for my playing of this masterpiece, all favorable, no critic has either noticed or mentioned the change!

A very interesting comparison of the two manners of playing the piano postlude of *Frauenliebe und Leben* can be had by first playing the Victor recording of the cycle, in which I play for Helen Traubel, followed by that of Isabelle French, with George Reeves accompanying.

My engagement to accompany a young singer, Klara Erler, in her debut recital in Berlin in 1903 unexpectedly brought about an opportunity to play for the greatest German violinist, Josef Joachim. It seems that the father of Klara Erler, of the music publishers Ries-Erler, was an intimate friend of Joachim, and the venerable artist had generously consented to appear as guest soloist on the program of his friend's daughter. In looking over the music in preparation for my task, it occurred to me that the compositions Joachim had selected would afford me scant opportunity to show my ability as an ensemble player. It was too great an occasion to be lost in accompanying lesser works, with a great master who was supreme in the classical repertoire. So I boldly wrote to Joachim

Program of Recital by Klara Erler

[135]

Postcard from Joseph Joachim

at the Hochschule, of which he was director, requesting him to consider the inclusion of a Mozart sonata on the program, in place of the selections he had made. To my astonished delight, Joachim responded by writing the opening violin passages of three of Mozart's sonatas for violin and piano on a postcard, telling me to take my choice. You may be sure that I made the most of the great opportunity!

Several years before the occasion of my first performance with Joachim, I had accompanied his wife, Amalie, a leading contralto of the day, at a concert in Berlin given in honor of the 60th anniversary of the birth of Max Bruch. The other artists on this program were Josef Hofmann and Teresa Carreño, playing a two piano composition, and Sarasate, the famous violin virtuoso!

Although Joachim seldom appeared as a soloist towards the close of his career, and I did not have occasion to accompany him again, he appeared at a later date as guest artist with a piano, violin, and 'cello ensemble which I founded in Berlin, *Das Holländische Trio*. Among my most treasured possessions is a letter written by Joachim concerning this group. This letter came into my possession many years after in a most curious way.

I had appeared as pianist for Emanuel Feuermann, the celebrated 'cellist, in Cologne. Some time afterwards, Feuermann purchased a collection of the Joachim letters. Among these, he found one that the violinist had written in response to an inquiry con-

SAAL BECHSTEIN.

Sonntag, den 2. Januar 1898, 12 Uhr

FEST-CONCERT

zur Feier des 60ten Geburtstages von

MAX BRUCH

geb. den 6. Januar 1838 zu Cöln a./Rh.

1. Gebet, a capella (aus op. 60).
   Mitglieder des Philharmonischen Chors unter Leitung des Herrn Siegfried Ochs.
2. Streichquartett No. II. in E-dur op. 10.
   Allegro maestoso — Andante quasi Adagio — Vivace ma non troppo — Finale Vivace.
   Die Herren Prof. Halir, Exner, Müller, Dechert.
3. Lieder:
   a) Verlassen, aus op. 17.
   b) Frage, aus op. 49
   c) Ungarisches Volkslied, aus op. 49.
   d) Carmosenella, aus op. 17.
   Frau Amalie Joachim und Herr Coenraad van Bos.
4. Fantasie für 2 Klaviere op. 11.
   Frau Teresa Carreño und Herr Josef Hofmann.
5. Palmsonntagmorgen, a capella (aus op. 60).
   Mitglieder d. Philh. Chors. Dir.: Herr S. Ochs.
6. I. Satz aus dem II. Violinconcert (D-moll op. 26.)
   Herr Pablo de Sarasate und Frau Berthe Marx-Goldschmidt.

Sämmtliche Compositionen von Max Bruch.

Program of Concert Honoring 60th Birthday of Max Bruch

Program of "Das Holländische Trio," with Joseph
Joachim and Emanuel Wirth as Assisting Artists

cerning *Das Holländische Trio*. That was in the early days of the Trio, and Joachim had not heard it play when he wrote the letter. It was a generous endorsement of the Trio, based upon familiarity with its reputation and personal knowledge of the capabilities of its members. Feuermann, realizing that this letter would be of peculiar interest to me, sent it to my daughter at Christmas time, with the request that it be placed under the tree with the other presents, as a surprise to me. This voice from the past is living evidence of the interest of one of the greatest artists of my time in the welfare and advancement of musicians of a younger generation. It was also indicative of the generous spirit of Emanuel Feuermann.

My first public playing with a 'cellist of eminence was with David Popper. Both his virtuosity and love of practical joking were so great that he was sometimes led into an exhibitionism derived as much from a confirmed sense of humor as from technical prowess. It was astonishing to me that an artist of such high attainments could stoop to musical pranks in a public concert. One occasion, in particluar, stands out in retrospect. As we were about to go on the stage, Popper turned to me abruptly and said: "Take care!" From this warning I knew he had some practical joke in mind, but *what*, I had no idea.

Wondering what would happen, I glanced through the score of the compositions we were about to play, his own *Vito*, for some sign of what was in store for me. Nor was I wrong in the expectation that

Program of Concert with Cellist David Popper

[141]

something out of the ordinary was about to happen. For, written in the music, was a word that had not been there at rehearsal. In my excitement I thought the word was *Stern*, or star. So I looked again to see if Popper had also drawn a star anywhere in the music, or for any other indication of what he had planned. All of this had taken place in the short interval between going on the stage and seating myself at the piano, where I glanced rapidly through the music while the venerable 'cellist responded to the acclaim of the audience.

But we were ready to begin the concert, and I determined to be on my guard and prepared for any eventuality. I started to play, fearful of the outcome. As I approached the word Popper had written in my score, I realized that what I had mistakenly read as *Stern* was *Sturm*, or storm. And as I came to a dominant 7th chord, where Popper had written the warning word, I realized that he had reached the point where he planned to carry out some colossal joke. Nor was I disappointed.

Coming to a dramatic pause, Popper then launched into the most extravagant improvisation of a cadenza that could be imagined, with recourse to *glissandi, double stops, harmonics,* and every cheap trick that might delight the musically illiterate—all in realistic imitation of a storm. It was to me, indeed, *Donnerwetter!* And I could not understand then, nor can I now, how an artist of the reputation of David

Popper could perpetrate such a tasteless joke upon a musical audience.

A very different type of virtuoso on the 'cello was Pablo Casals. Because of the hairless rotundity of both of our heads, a critic in Oxford, Ohio, after I had accompanied Casals in a concert in that city, wrote that, when we came on the stage together, he "wondered where the third billiard ball was." However, by recollections of association with this consummate artist are not primarily of a humorous nature.

After accompanying Casals at a concert in Cassel, Germany, he asked me if I could play for him two weeks later in Budapest. I replied that I would be very happy to do so, but that I must return to my home in Berlin in the interim, and that he probably would not want to pay the fee I would ask to travel from Berlin to Budapest, for one concert only. Casals then asked how much I would require for the trip and concert, and I told him: "700 marks." He immediately agreed to this, so I made the trip to Budapest.

The manager of Casal's concert on this occasion was known for double-dealing with artists. Casals, being forewarned, refused to perform until his entire fee of 7000 kronen was paid in advance. The night of the concert there was a sold out house; the audience had filled the hall; the scheduled hour for the performance had arrived. Casals refused to go on the stage. The manager pleaded. But Casals was adamant. Finally the manager came to Casals offering one half of the fee in cash, the other half by cheque. He said that one half of the amount was all the money he had on hand.

During these negotiations, the audience had become restive, and we could hear scattered applause and noise from some of those in the auditorium calling for the concert to start. The manager was becoming redfaced and flustered. As the scoundrel entreated Casals to begin, the great 'cellist showed the most remarkable poise under such circumstances that I have ever witnessed. He sat, the picture of coolness and calmness, playing scales—while the manager stormed and raged without avail. Casals had had a similar disagreeable experience in Karlsruhe, and he was not to be swayed by promises.

Finally the manager, now desperate, said that the president of the bank was in the hall, and would guarantee the cheque for one half the fee. At that, Casals said: "Get the bank president." Soon the official arrived and Casals told him his story. The president said: "I do not know whether the cheque is good or bad. But, in any event, I will guarantee the amount and will see that you are paid."

It was now three quarters of an hour past the time scheduled for the concert. The sounds from the hall had been increasing in volume. But in the midst of all the confusion and excitement, Casals had kept on playing scales, quite unperturbed. And, now that the delay was over, he appeared on the stage where the audience received him tumultuously. The first number was a difficult Bach Sonata for solo 'cellist.

Under perfect control, showing no signs of the recent conflict, Casals, from the first note, played with the complete poise and mastery that makes him such a consummate artist.

Soon after the first world war, I happened to be on a Dutch ship coming to the United States from Europe. That extraordinary artist and woman, Ernestine Schumann-Heink, was aboard. The story of the conflict of emotions this great singer had suffered during the war is well known. She had become an American citizen and had lived for many years in her dearly beloved adopted country. But she had had sons in both the German and American military service. In fact, she was bringing back the widow and children of a son, an officer on a German U-boat, who had been a war casualty. Her solicitude for her grandchildren and their mother was very touching.

After the custom of trans-Atlantic trips, a concert was planned. I was placed in charge of the program. A survey of the artistic resources on board disclosed a choral group made up of members of a society of Swiss teachers; I was to do the accompanying; and Madame Schumann-Heink was to bring the concert to a close.

It will be recalled that the performance of music with German text, and frequently of music by German composers, had been out of favor during the first world war, and had not yet, in 1919, been resumed. It is not necessary to discuss here the misguided actions of many, and the bitter, unthinking emotions and acts which were aroused and instigated during that time of stress. But the fact that similar bitterness against the genius of a people, and particularly the dead masters of past eras, who belong to all mankind, irrespective of time or boundaries, did not arise during the recent conflict, shows that, in general, people have learned a lesson in the unreasonableness and futility of such reactions.

But at the time of which I am speaking, 1918, it was simply out of the question to perform music with German texts. So when the Swiss singers presented me with a list of their songs, to appear on the printed programs, I was horrified to read such titles as *Du, Deutscher Rhein, Mein Vaterland, und so weiter*. Schumann-Heink, realizing the delicacy of the situation, had planned to sing an Italian aria and songs in English. Not knowing what to do and not wishing to offend the Swiss teachers, who to be sure were "German-Swiss," I asked Schumann-Heink what she would advise. With characteristic resourcefulness and courage, she quickly responded: "Leave it to me. Do not print the names of the songs. Simply state on the program that the Swiss Singing Society will sing a group of songs. Before they sing, I shall make an announcement."

The evening of the concert, Madame Schumann-Heink arose and said: "You are going to hear a group of songs by the Swiss Singing Society. The language in which they sing sounds like German. But it is not German! *Please don't shoot them!*" Whereupon they sang, in the plainest German, *Mein Vaterland* and *Du, Deutscher Rhein.* The concert was a great success, and if anyone was the wiser, nothing was said.

Shortly after this Schumann-Heink sang in Newark, N. J. For the first time, after the war, she included German *Lieder* by Brahms, purposely as a final group on the program. The audience numbered some 4000 people. Just prior to beginning the closing group, Schumann-Heink announced: "The war is over. The time to sing German songs is here. If there are any in the audience who do not wish to hear them, they may leave now."

And quietly, without demonstration, about 200 people left the auditorium.

CHAPTER X

CONSIDERING THE PUBLIC

THE true functions of the accompanist extend to such important matters as the art of program making. The informed instrumentalist can be of invaluable assistance in this respect, for many singers are concerned primarily with the problems of vocalization. If the final choice devolves upon them, the danger of committing errors of taste and failure to achieve musical balance in program building are only too frequently to be witnessed.

One of the commonest errors is that of women artists singing songs the texts of which are specifically and solely appropriate for male singers. Curiously enough, this defect of judgment is more often encountered with women than with men. No man would ever think of attempting a public performance of Schumann's song cycle, *Frauenliebe und Leben*. Yet many women sing Brahms' *Minnelied, Botschaft, O liebliche Wangen*, and Schumann's *Aufträge*. A careful study of the texts of these songs will show conclusively that they were never intended to be performed by women. The thoughts and emotions implicit in the poems are suited only to male singers.

On the other hand, for similar reasons, Brahms' *Der Schmied* is a woman's song and should never be sung by a man.

It will be observed that most serenades, or *Ständchen*, are men's songs. This applies to both the *Ständchen* of Schubert and that by Richard Strauss. These are among the commonest examples of errors of taste in choosing songs for public performance. That they go virtually unnoticed by both the public and critics does not relieve the performers of responsibility in a fundamental esthetic principle.

The matter of the appropriate selection of songs for male and female singers was frequently stressed by the great vocal teacher, Julius Stockhausen. While he was able to and did sing all *Lieder* for his pupils, he was adamant in adherence to this mentioned esthetic principle, more honored in the breach than in the observance.

Consideration for the audience should be a major factor in the arrangement of programs. Anything that tends towards monotony is to be avoided. Two songs of similar mood should never be placed in close juxtaposition. The same rule applies to keys. Two songs in the same key are not to be placed side by side. Similarly, I have always avoided the performance, in sequence, of two songs in minor keys.

But the rules for program arrangement, in which the element of variety dominates, are not merely to be comprehended through negation. They may be expressed positively, and be extended to include the choice of accompaniments. When the accompanist has the opportunity of aiding in choosing songs for a program, he should take advantage of it to see that some selections are included which show his capabilities in favorable light. This adds zest to the occasion and affords a contrast very important to musical enjoyment and audience reaction.

In recommending songs for inclusion in the repertoire of the singer, it is advisable occasionally to suggest a song or cycle in which the accompanist is afforded opportunity to display his musicality and pianism to good advantage. Such a choice is highly to be recommended in Chausson's *Poème de l'amour et de la mer,* a cycle of great beauty, a part only of which is familiar to most singers. If performed in its entirety, as it should be, it furnishes a rare opportunity for the proficient accompanist to do some very beautiful playing. This cycle includes an interlude for piano solo. I have found that it lends effectiveness to the interlude if the singer stands informally in the embrasure of the piano, resting an elbow on the instrument, in an attitude of attentive listening. So simple and natural a procedure saves the singer from the necessity of standing and facing the audience, while waiting for the pianist to finish. It also, as I have discovered, influences the audience in concentration on the psychological unfolding of Chausson's masterpiece, without a break in continuity.

I have spoken of the many considerations for the soloist, as well as the music, which must constantly actuate the accompanist who would function most effectively. The matter of "consideration for the audience" must be omnipresent, in both the choice of material and the manner of its presentation. A few instances, illustrating basic principles, will serve to indicate the direction in which "the manner of presentation" must be channeled, if the undeviating attention and musical interest of the audience are to be maintained.

The first of these has to do with those moments in which the accompanist plays a phrase alone, the same phrase to be repeated by the singer, *molto legato*. Such a moment should be a foreshadowing of that smooth sustaining of a melodic line which is the very basis of the singer's style and vocal equipment. Its attainment is much more difficult on the piano. I have found it advisable to condition myself psychologically for the execution of such phrases by saying to myself: "Now I must show the singer how she must sing *legato*. The melody must flow from the piano as if from inner necessity." And I listen with the same intensity to myself first and to the singer afterwards, to see if this has been realized. Without this intense listening, the desired result will never be ideally attained. Its consummation produces a living musical quality that unites everyone within earshot, who is capable of sensitive response, in that magic union of music, artists, and audience which is the ultimate goal of all music-making. It is the very essence of musical experience.

The first example I have chosen occurs in Schumann's song cycle, *Dichterliebe*, in the course of the *Lied, Ich hab' in Traum geweinet*. The accompanist plays a phrase:

Example 1

This is followed by the singing of the same melody by the soloist:

Example 2

Similarly, in the 23rd *Lied* of Schubert's *Winterreise* (*Die Nebensonnen*), the piano introduction (Example I) must be played in such a melodic expressive manner as fairly to inspire the soloist to sing in the same style, when executing the repetition of the phrase which follows in Example II:

[152]

Example 1
Nicht zu langsam

Example 2

Drei Son-nen sah-ich am Him-mel steh'n, hab' lang' und fest sie

The accompanist, in other words, must not be content with emulating the *bel canto* of the singer, but should, at least in his own mind, take the lead in supplying the ideal musical sustaining of a melodic line, if the full power and beauty of the music are to be projected to the audience.

Another important consideration on the difficult subject of the interaction of audience and music is related to songs in which sustained power is demanded. An excellent example of this occurs in the last two pages of Schubert's *Gretchen am Spinnrade*, in which the singer is called upon to execute a climax of cumulative intensity. Although a steady *crescendo* is indicated in the music, such a rendition would be equally unfair to music, singer, and audience, and would result in an anti-climax, rather than in the desired building up to a height.

The reason for this is to be found in natural laws, whose procedures are not dissimilar to those of art, or *vice versa*. In observing the gradually cumulative rise in the waves at the seashore, you have probably noticed that there is not a steadily maintained increase in intensity, or *crescendo*, but a series of rises, each succeeding one greater, until the highest crest has been reached. Each rise is followed by a recession, but the whole series results in a cumulative sequence, conveying the impression of inevitably expanding power, which is the essential quality of climax. Similar effect is witnessed in a series of foothills leading up to a dominating peak.

Since "all-climax" would result in "no-climax," or anti-climax, the effect of constantly sustained power would inevitably result in a nullification of the musical intent. It would also defeat the singer's purpose. Furthermore, it would demand a sustaining of interest and attention on the part of auditors which is contrary to both natural laws and the tenets of art—not to mention human endurance. Therefore, a careful study of the final pages of Schubert's *Gretchen am Spinnrade* will show that the desired and appropriate musical result will be attained in breaking the monotony inherent in a steadily maintained increase in volume, by beginning phrases with a slightly lessened intensity from the volume attained at the end of the preceding phrases, being careful to maintain an interrelationship of musical expansion which furnishes both the necessary relief, or recession, and the desired climax.

The strain of singing so strenuous a song as *Gretchen am Spinnrade* on tour, several times a week, with other songs of similar difficulty on the same program, has led me to advise against the placing of too many songs of a physically taxing nature on programs chosen for extended tours. This is a simple justice, not only to the singers but to the public which pays for and deserves only the best. No singer is able to maintain a constantly high standard when subjected to unduly protracted strain, night after night.

Not all of the efforts to please the public devolve upon the soloist. The accompanist must always keep in mind the responsibility of adequate projection of his tone into the auditorium in which he happens to perform. This depends upon many factors, including size of the hall, acoustical properties, the instrument, as well as the size of the audience. The variability is so constant that I have found it advisable to ask someone in the audience to listen carefully and inform me at certain intervals during the program whether my playing is balanced with the soloist; whether it is too loud or too soft.

The necessity for depending upon other ears than my own in order to adapt my playing to various auditoriums and audiences was impressed upon me as early as April of 1896, when I played my first concert in the great hall of the Philharmonie, in Berlin, with

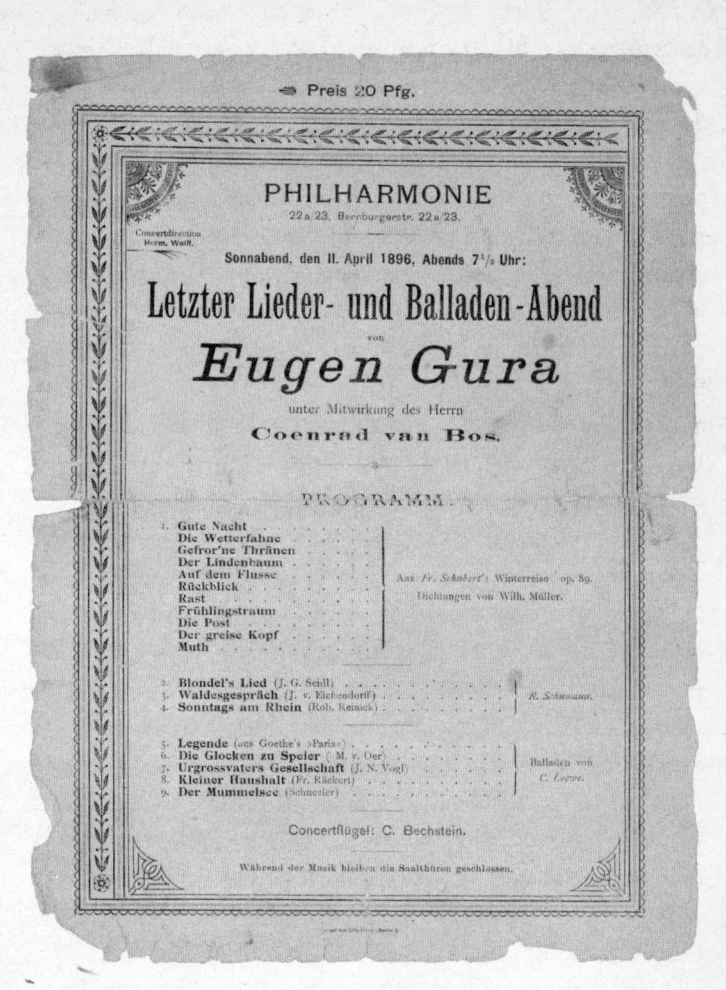

Program of Recital by Eugen Gura

Eugen Gura, the celebrated *Lieder* singer. I asked a musical friend to report the effect of my playing at the first opportunity. During a break in the middle of Gura's first long group, my friend came backstage and said my playing would gain by being louder. Again he reported at the end of the group, saying it was improved, but could still stand more tone. Finally, after the second group, the friend reported: "Now your playing is exactly right! Everyone in the audience is talking about it."

From that time until today, I have had absolutely no trouble getting engagements in my chosen field as professional accompanist.

Although the accompanist may not always be forewarned of the peculiar difficulties of playing in a particular hall, there is one important consideration in which he should never be taken by surprise. This is the matter of especially difficult accompaniments in the standard repertoire, which he will most certainly be called upon to play. It is indispensable that the pianist master such accompaniments before they are first placed before him by a singer. The following represents a list of suggested songs which should be "in the repertoire" of every competent accompanist:

Der Erlkönig . . . . *Schubert*

Cäcilie
Schlechtes Wetter
Frühlingsfeier

Lied des Steinklopfers
Des Dichters Abendgang
Der Arbeitsmann .... *Richard Strauss*

Ganymed
An eine Aeolsharfe
Lied von Winde
Der Rattenfänger
Waldmädchen
Prometheus
Abschied .... *Hugo Wolf*

Blinde Kuh
Vier Ernste Gesänge
Sommernacht .... *Brahms*

While the foregoing list by no means embraces all of the difficult songs which might embarrass the accompanist unfamiliar with their technical and musical demands, it is indicative of a serious need of which many in the profession become aware when it is too late.

In considering matters of importance in the interrelation of artists and public, both with the idea in mind of giving the utmost in artistry and of awakening appropriate response, I am impelled to broach a subject, however briefly, which is generally treated by soloists without due consideration for the esthetic principles involved. This is the moot subject of singing songs in translation. It is an essential consideration for all program making, and one in which the matter of public appeal should take first place.

I am in complete disagreement with those who advocate the singing of *Lieder* or other songs only in the original languages of their texts. It is of prime importance that the words of songs be articulate to the audience. But there exists the custom in America of singing all songs by foreign composers in foreign languages. This has led all too frequently to fantastic situations. For instance, one hears Grieg's *Ein Schwan* sung most often in German. It happens that Hans Schmidt made an excellent German translation of the text of this song, originally in Norwegian. But if it is to be sung in America, *in translation*, why not in English? It should either be sung in the original Norwegian, in which case few would understand its words, or in English, in which it would become intelligible to everyone in an American audience. In the first instance it would conform to the esthetic opinion of some that all songs should be performed in their original tongues; in the second, it would aid, through intelligibility, in conveying the full meaning of a work of art to everyone. No matter what the excellence of the German translation, I see no reason for singing it in that language to an American audience.

In the case of Tschaikowsky's *Nur Wer die Sehnsucht Kennt*, its performance in German is understandable, since the original was a poem by Goethe. However, it has justly become widely known to the American public as *None but the Lonely Heart*. But other songs of Dvorák, Grieg, Tschaikowsky, Sinding, Rachmaninoff, and Sibelius, written for the greater part to texts in their native tongues, are frequently heard in translations other than English—mostly in German and French. I believe this to show a lack of consideration for American audiences, as well as being esthetically false.

The argument usually advanced against singing songs in English versions is that the translations are, generally speaking, very poor. However, I recall some years ago that an Australian singer by the name of Illingworth gave recitals in America, singing all songs in excellent translations he had made himself. He immediately attracted much attention, but did not enjoy a protracted success, as a public which was at first intrigued by an interesting and much-needed experiment, later lost interest because of amusement at his Australian pronunciation.

At a later date, the distinguished soprano, Florence Easton, demonstrated conclusively the high degree of artistry that could be attained in songs in which excellent English translations are used. And many years ago Walter Damrosch was responsible for performances of Wagner's *Die Meistersinger* in English translation, at the Metropolitan, in which the audience was heard to laugh at the right time, and for understandable reason!

While discussing the consideration due the public by concert artists, I cannot refrain from paying my compliments to those persons who, with misguided zeal, endeavor to impose themselves upon soloists during the course of a concert. Needless to say, singers, especially, are under considerable strain when appearing before audiences. They subject themselves to a thorough self-discipline which gives them the outward appearance of ease. However, constant public appearance scarcely mitigates the tension indissolubly linked with performance. This must be considered a normal state with all sensitive artists. In order to protect singers from encroachment upon their privacy during recital by well-meaning but thoughtless admirers, I stand by the door of the artist's room in the intervals between groups, as well as during the intermission, and inform all comers that the soloist may not be seen until after the concert. This procedure forestalls possibility of any contingency which might upset the artist's composure through the additional strain of carrying on conversation, particularly with strangers.

During the course of these discussions, I have endeavored to present the principal factors involved in the training and development of the proficient accompanist, as I see him from the vantage point of more than fifty years of continuous public experience. The obligations of the worthy accompanist are very great, both to the artists with whom he performs and to the public. But the arduous work, constant service, and great responsibilities are amply justified by rich musical experiences and human associations. While these are the true compensations of the accompanist, I shall close with a very practical consideration. Young accompanists at the outset of their professional careers frequently ask me how they can get started. Fortunately, the opportunities for those properly equipped are not lacking, and the course to pursue is not a difficult one.

All of the music journals carry many advertisements of vocal teachers and coaches. My advice to the young accompanist is to write to these vocal instructors, outlining his or her qualifications. Similar communications may be sent to dance studios and instrumentalists who require accompanists. In this way opportunities may be uncovered not only for accompanying in the studios but for various students of the teachers, who frequently require the services of accompanists in studio work, private practice, or professional appearances. The field of opportunity for the well-tempered accompanist is constantly expanding. The only limitations are self-imposed.

RECORDINGS BY COENRAAD V. BOS

No.	Title	Composer
V-7794	Auf dem Kirchhofe Das Mädchen Spricht Vergebliches Ständchen	
V-7795	Erlaube Mir Feinsliebchen, du sollst Mein Mädel hat 'nen Rosenmund Wie komm' ich denn zur Tür herein	Brahms
V-7793	Feldeinsamkeit Die Nachtigall Ständchen	
V-6755	Immer leiser wird mein Schlummer Von Ewiger Liebe	
VM-737	Fraunliebe und Leben (With Elena Gerhardt)	Schumann

Hugo Wolf Society Albums (HMV)

Vol. I	With Elena Gerhardt
Vol. II	With Alexandre Trianti
Vol. III	With Gerhard Hüsch
Vol. IV	With Elisabeth Rethberg and Alexander Kipnis

No.	Title	Composer
V-6881	Frühlingstraum	
V-6846	Gute Nacht	
V-6838	Der Leiermann	Schubert
V-6846	Der Lindenbaum	
V-6881	Wasserfluth	
V-6838	Der Wegweiser	

A bibliography of recordings by other artists mentioned in this book may be obtained from the publisher.

V = RCA-Victor; VM = RCA-Victor Masterwork Album; HMV = His Master's Voice (England).